Overcoming Shame, Finding Freedom:

Healing For Sexual Abuse and Trauma.

Overcoming Shame, Finding Freedom:

Healing For Sexual Abuse and Trauma.

Written by Cherry Fargo

Published in the United States of America

Endorsements

"Are you suffering from the trauma of sexual abuse? Do you know and love someone who is? Are you looking for someone who has successfully walked this path? Cherry herself knows the shame and pain victims carry. She also knows that there is freedom and healing. Her easy-to-understand guidance comes from her experiences - the trauma, the resistance, the healing, and the wholeness. She is the encouraging friend you need to hear so you know you are not alone. Whether you are a teen, an adult, or a grandparent, Cherry's tender words will help you know the next steps to take. Let her help you or the one you love to exchange your shame and pain for freedom and wholeness."

~ Rene Shelton

M.Ed., Licensed Professional Counselor-Supervisor

Through sharing her own story of sexual abuse and her journey of finding healing in Christ, Cherry Fargo gives us the tools to help transform the negative effects of sexual abuse and equip us to reclaim our identity and our stories. Overcoming Shame, Finding Freedom will definitely be a resource in my toolbox to be used in ministry.

~Teri Beane

Author and Women's Minister

I have had the honor of friendship with Cherry for over 20 years. I am so grateful she decided to document her healing so others could draw from her strength. This story is now a testimony of the power we have in God, to heal our trauma and restore our hope. Cherry Fargo writes an anthem against our enemy pursuing our destruction and provides an effective weapon to defeat him. I pray everyone struggling against the bondage of this kind of pain, trusts and believes God is able, and willing to heal.

~ Chaplain Lisa Harper-Lerner

Author, National Speaker,

Founder of Bless the Badge Ministries

What a wonderfully written and practical resource for those seeking freedom and wholeness from traumatic abuse. Cherry's personal stories were so relatable, and I appreciate that there was nothing graphically depicted...only HOPE!

~D.J. May Hejtmanek
Writer and Artist

This book is an incredible tool for survivors and those who are walking alongside them, as well as anyone looking for practical strategies on retraining their brain from various stress responses. It includes useful stories and helpful steps for finding freedom in Christ and releasing shame, and I especially appreciated the sections on self-labeling, spiritual pearls, and reacting vs responding. As a former foster mom who has walked with kids through trauma responses, as well as someone walking through my own challenges with fear and anxiety, I found this book immensely practical and a great blueprint for healing. Cherry's gracious approach is based in science and easy to understand, a good resource to use in a small group with trusted friends and confidants, and a great reference book to return back to again and again as you journey forward in finding healing and restoration in relationship with Jesus.

~Cindy M. Knight
Advocate, Artist, and Author of Gospel Hope Journal

Acknowledgements

This book would in no way be possible without Granny. I am deeply grateful that she has always believed in doing what needed to be done to take care of family. Her intuition, ability to discern the truth, and her fortitude to intervene surely saved me.

I'd like to express my deepest gratitude to my husband Shannon for the decades of reminders to "write the book!" Twenty-eight years of marriage haven't always been easy, but I wouldn't trade any of it for the world. I couldn't ask for a better champion, supporter, friend, or spouse. Thank you for always pushing me to pursue the dream. You're my hero!

Dianna, I appreciate you for being a friend when most would not, for always accepting me for who I was and who I am, for looking past my outward appearances during my years of abuse and seeing me. Life would have been truly unbearable without a friend during that time.

Dad, thank you for taking me to church when I was young and giving me the opportunity to know Jesus.

Thank you, Marquez Family, for being a safe place to land. I wish I had been able to express my gratitude better in the years I spent with you.

Teri Beane, I extend my heartfelt thankfulness to you for being a sounding board and cheerleader, for praying with me and offering not just your lake house, but your gift of hospitality for a writing retreat to work on this book. Those few days free of distractions were exactly what I needed to get moving in the right direction.

Christine Beatty and Donna Smith, thank you for the two years of prayer counseling that finally brought healing and hope into focus. My time spent with you ladies was foundational for the concepts presented on these pages.

Mike Lehew, I am grateful for the foreword you wrote, for the encouragement and support you have extended, for your prayers, friendship, and godly leadership. I am so thankful God brought us to Church Inside Out. You are appreciated!

To all my Church Inside Out, New Life Church, and Bethel Temple friends and family, thank you for your prayers and discipleship over the years. My spiritual growth and development are due in part to the nurturing I have experienced in fellowship with you. God deserves all the glory for who I have become and all I have accomplished. I am grateful for all the times He revealed Himself to me through you.

To Danielle Wilson, Patty Loredo, Deanna Payne, and the many other women who were willing to share their stories: I have heard your amazing testimonies of triumph and healing and truly been inspired by them. Thank you for your transparency, input, and encouragement.

D.J. May Hejtmanek, Rene Shelton, Cindy Knight, and Lisa Lerner, I appreciate the content consulting, endorsements, proofreading, and affirmations that I had written the book I set out to write. Thank you for lending me your eyes and your perspectives.

For the team of service providers that I could not have finished this without, you rock! Thank you, Crystal Ifekoya of BOSS Encounters, Dee Selby of Format My Stuff, and Sara Geringer, Book Launch Manager.

Finally, to my children, you have been the catalyst for my desire to find wholeness. I can only hope that my efforts to provide you with a stable home and upbringing have been meaningful and encouraging to you all. I'm so proud of each of you. Love you bunches!

Many blessings and much love to you all,
Cherry

Table of Contents

Introduction

Navigating the Better Way

Identity

Discovering Your Specific Purpose

Dedication

For my mom and my sister
and every other woman
who has experienced the heartache
of sexual abuse and trauma
directly and indirectly.

Foreword

I remember meeting Cherry a few years ago when she showed up at our church. The words that come to my mind as I got to know her during the next several weeks and months: humble, prayer warrior, confident, compassionate, passionate, and spiritually driven. She exuded a humble confidence and was a passionate person of prayer that wanted to help others find and know Christ. But behind all of this, I couldn't help but think that she had a story.

I wasn't sure what her history was, but I knew she had been through a lot. Over the course of the next few years, she shared her survivor story. I thought, "How does someone survive such abuse? How does someone who has gone through so much find freedom and exhibit those characteristics that Cherry had shown?" I noticed there was such a peace and a calm about Cherry, in spite of it all.

How in the world was she able to have such peace? At some point on her journey, she was able to "demolish and clear the debris of trauma." It came with an intentional decision to allow God to remake her into who He had created her to be.

But...that process was hard, and that process took years. Even so, God used those years of walking with Him to show others how to heal from horrendous abuse. Cherry, in her incredible way, helps survivors clear the path to help them find freedom from fear, guilt and shame and understand their God given identity and purpose.

Her words will also assist those who have not personally experienced abuse know how to direct and guide those who have been abused. For me, as a pastor, her timely words couldn't come in a better season to help me know how to minister to those who have been abused.

Cherry has written a timely book that is much needed in a day when abuse is rampant. We need more tools like this one to help us address how to walk alongside people who are hurting and need healing. Overcoming Shame: Finding Freedom is a timely, practical, and life-giving work.

In your hands, you hold the story of how one life was remade, and my prayer is the same thing that Cherry prayed in this book, "That you will be able to demolish and clear the debris of trauma quickly and embrace the process of being remade into who God created you to be."

Today, Cherry serves as our prayer coordinator for our church. It's because of her journey and God working through her that she has the ability to help so many others.

Thank you, Cherry, for being open and honest and having the desire to help others find freedom!

Mike Lehew, Executive Director of Mobile Missions Network
& Lead Missionary of Church Inside Out

Preface

Prom. I loved going to formal dances in the years following the abuse I experienced. Each one I went to offered me the opportunity to feel as if I had risen above the trauma I had been subjected to for two years. My junior prom was especially memorable. I wore a spectacular black fitted gown, had a very handsome date, and went to a phenomenally posh restaurant for a pre-dance dinner. My best friend and I double dated with a couple of young men who were also best friends. And of course, half the school population had chosen the same location to eat as well.

As young ladies do, my friend and I excused ourselves to go to the restroom. As we stepped from the flooring that was carpeted to a tile floor, there was a distinct absence of a wet floor sign. I continued strolling confidently in the direction of the ladies' room when all of the sudden I found myself on the floor. But not for long, I was up and on my feet in a split second, pushing away those who were trying to help me. I didn't want anyone to notice what had happened.

Upon entering the bathroom, I discovered that my dress that had been slit to my knee was now very inappropriately slit all the way to my hip. As I was taking stock of the damage and brainstorming a solution, a maître d' came to the rescue with a sewing kit. She stitched the seam back together and my dress seemed like new. As we returned to our table, my hopes that no one had noticed were quickly dashed. I think my date was the first to crack jokes with "have a nice trip?" and "see you next fall!" We laughed about it, went on with the evening and had a great time.

Overcoming shame and finding freedom after sexual abuse is a lot like having your feet knocked out from under you. There is a tendency to jump up from the trauma, push away the help in hopes no one will notice, and go back to living life as normally as possible. Although, there is usually damage from the fall that cannot be ignored or so easily fixed as a dress seam.

The healing journey is one that takes time and effort and even help. My hope is that just as the maître d' assisted me in repairing the damage to my gown, this book will assist many women in finding hope, freedom, purpose and identity in the aftermath of abuse. Are you one of those women? You might be, or you might know of someone who is.

This book is for all women who have experienced sexual abuse, sexual assault, sex trafficking, and any related trauma from those events. It marries the practical applications of restoration with spiritual truths and provides a framework to move survivors towards hope and healing.

It is for the woman who has struggled to overcome her past due to limited resources, support, or knowledge. It is for the woman questioning her faith because of the wounds she incurred at the hands of others. It is for the woman who longs to know her true identity and purpose in a life after abuse, and it is for the woman who wants to live victoriously.

Sexual abuse rarely just affects the victim. Those who love someone who has been abused also feel the weight of what happened. Trauma is like a bomb. Not only does it destroy what it sits on, but it damages everything around it. Some relatives and family members of those abused will also be impacted by the victim's trauma. They may also carry their own wounds of guilt and shame for not recognizing what was going on or disbelieving what they were told. Because this book addresses how to overcome shame, it is for those individuals as well.

While I have avoided being graphic and minimized my use of specific details about my abuse in writing this, I have been very transparent. Some of what you read may make you feel uncomfortable. I did not shy away from that because abuse is an uncomfortable topic, period. With the exception of a few general details I have shared, I have chosen to focus more on the feelings of shame and despair nearly every victim encounters and can relate to. In my experience, shame is the biggest barrier to overcoming what is suffered at the hands of abusers. Therefore, this book is aimed at providing a framework for overcoming that shame and finding freedom.

As I work towards the publication of this book, I have been asked about how long it has taken to write it. The real answer is nearly all my life. However, putting the words onto paper began in the fall of 2019 but was then put on hold after facing one loss after another in 2020. One of those losses was the death of my mom in late 2020. After her passing it was difficult for me to start on this project again, because as much as this is for every survivor who reads it, it was for her as well. The thought of her never getting to see the fullness of my complete freedom has been heartbreaking and feeling like she would have also found healing in the pages of what I have written is just bittersweet.

In the pages of this work, you will discover the procedures that have helped me find my own freedom and purpose. It has been hard won and taken decades. If I can help anyone move through the steps to wholeness more quickly than I did by sharing my experiences, then all the time and effort in completing the process is well worth it.

I have found journaling to be a great practice that helped me put things in perspective and therefore have included journaling prompts for you at the end of each chapter. There is space for you to jot down your responses, but you may prefer to have a separate notebook to record your thoughts as you reflect on what you are remembering and learning. Even if you do not write out your answers, I encourage you to take some time to think about the prompts as a means to help you process what you have been reading.

That being said, this book is not meant to be prescriptive or diagnostic for anyone's specific situation. The details of what you endured will have similarities to what others have experienced but also be specifically unique to you at the same time. Please use this book as a tool to help move you forward on your quest for wholeness but also consider other resources too. Counseling and life coaching can be valuable implements as you seek to be free from your dark past and step into a bright future.

Asking for help does not belittle you in any way. Some burdens are far too heavy to bear on our own. It is better to have support than try to maneuver these challenges alone. No matter how many times you get your feet knocked out from underneath you, let me encourage you to get back up! Regardless of how long it takes or how hard it is to walk through the process of restoration, it is worth it! I pray you find the courage to do the hard work!

~Cherry Fargo, Tulsa Metro Area, Oklahoma, 2023

"Courage doesn't always roar.
Sometimes courage is the quiet voice
at the end of the day saying,
'I will try again tomorrow.'"
~Mary Anne Radmacher

Introduction

1.

A Starting Place

Long before mp3 players, cell phones, and digital music, cassette tapes supplied us with our favorite tunes, one of the coolest ways to listen to our music was by blaring it from a boombox. Rectangular in shape with an AM/FM radio, the boom box usually had a cassette player located in the center and on either end of it were speakers. Making it even more amazing was the fact that it was portable. In addition to having a wall plug, it could also be powered by batteries which meant we could take it with us to a friend's house, the park, the beach, or just any old place you wanted to go. It was just the right size for carrying on your shoulder which was of course what we did. In the days of too big bangs, preppy shirts, penny loafers, denim jackets, banana clips and heavy metal hair bands, this was revolutionary, and it was just so cool to have a boombox.

You might think then that getting a boom box for Christmas would be one of my best childhood memories, but it's not. My mom was so excited for me to open that gift. We didn't have a lot of money, so I know it was a sacrifice for her to buy it for me. And because it was a pricier gift, it was the one and only one I received that year. The problem was that I knew exactly what I was getting ahead of time, and I didn't want to disappoint my mom by not acting surprised and elated. It was a gift every 13-year-old should have loved. To further complicate the matter, I was worried that if I didn't act as excited as I would have been if I was surprised, she would want to know why, and that terrified me.

The assumption that maybe I had snooped to find out what my presents were and that I was afraid of the repercussions would seem like a logical one, but I loved fun surprises. I still do. The unfortunate truth is that my stepfather was an abusive man. The gift was a "bribe" aimed at getting me to cooperate with him for "play" time. That is what he called it when he sexually molested me. I didn't have a choice though; if I refused, the punishment would have been harsh. I would have been assigned numerous chores and grounded from the few freedoms I had.

I wouldn't have been the only one to suffer either. My brother would also be assigned extra work for no reason and subjected to an onslaught of physical and verbal abuse. The verbal abuse would be aimed at my mother once she got home from work too. It was really a lose / lose scenario for me that happened often, almost weekly, over the course of two years. And the threats to kill me if I ever told anyone about "play" time kept me silent.

Fear wasn't the only deterrent to sharing this dark secret though. Fear was accompanied by his friend Shame. I was so overcome by shame that I could not enjoy the gift my mother genuinely and sincerely wanted me to have. She had no idea what was going on or that she had been manipulated into buying something that had been offered to me as a bargaining chip. I wanted to love the gift, but I hated it. Bitter disappointment at not getting any other presents that I might have enjoyed simply intensified the guilt I was feeling. In addition, there was this dark secret that I was not only keeping but felt compelled to protect. I'd heard often enough that I wouldn't be believed even if I did tell and my vague pleas for help at school had already been dismissed as weird and dramatic. Fear and Shame had become the identity I had assumed and kept me from freedom.

The following spring, my maternal grandmother planned a party for my birthday at her house. She invited my cousins and my only friend from school. At one point during the evening when Granny and I were alone, she asked about the bruise on my cheek. I had gotten it when my stepfather threw a bottle of gun oil across the room at me out of anger. Granny pressed with questions about how else I might have been mistreated and was there any inappropriate touching going on. After two horrible years of abuse, the secret came out. Although I said very little, my tears confirmed her concerns and suspicions.

I can't imagine how difficult it must have been for my grandmother to call my mother and reveal to her the horror of what my life had been like. My Granny has always been a woman of exceptional grit, but it must have been heartbreaking for her to tell her only daughter the sickening truth and then dictate to her that I would not be returning home. My mom arrived sometime later with several trash bags that had been quickly packed with my belongings and her own arsenal of questions she wanted answered. She was looking for details that might somehow confirm the truth, but the fear and shame were so great I could not bring myself to share them with her.

I am sure my mother was overwhelmed by what was happening. She was pregnant with her youngest child, my youngest brother. I also had a baby sister, Tammy, who was nearly three. She and the baby on the way were both the biological children of my stepfather. My brother, who was a couple years younger than me, and I shared a different father than my youngest siblings. Mom was doing the best she knew how to care for our family, but she left that night not believing the accusations she had heard. She did, however, fear what might happen to any one of us, and especially me, if I returned home with her or if the authorities were involved. So, I was left in the safety of my grandmother's care but even though the greatest source of my fear was no longer an imminent threat, its echoes rang in the depths of my being, and I was overwhelmed by shame.

If only we had known then that I wasn't my stepfather's only victim. Unfortunately, he was also sexually molesting my sister. Her abuse wasn't discovered until after my mother separated from him two years later, when my sister was six. Initially we thought that maybe her abuse began when I was removed from the home. My teenage self felt responsible; maybe if I had hid the secret better she would have been spared, maybe I could have protected her. It was quite a while before we discovered he had been molesting her since she was only a year old, that our abuse began about the same time. As soon as what had been happening to her was revealed, in an effort to help her through the healing process, it was shared with her that her father had also abused me.

Sometime after she heard my story, she entered my room and sat down on my bed with what seemed like the weight of the world on her shoulders. The eleven years that separated us did nothing to lessen the unjust sense of responsibility she seemed to feel. With grief and remorse, the words "I'm so sorry for the things my daddy did to you" spilled out of her mouth. My heart broke. We both felt responsible somehow for things we had no control over. This is the false shame Satan attempts to heap upon us to strip away our freedom, identity, and purpose.

I wish I could say that the journey to reclaiming identity and walking in purpose went quickly and smoothly for both my sister and me. Unfortunately, fear and shame kept Tammy and me both immobilized for far too long, but in different ways. My biological father had taken me to church when I was young, and I believed in Jesus because of it. However, after the conversation with my sister in my room that day, I became angry at God. I just could not fathom how God could allow such evil to happen to a baby. I was furious about what happened to my sister and walked away from God for a decade. I wouldn't even acknowledge that there was a god. Tammy struggled almost her entire life with multiple personality disorder, bi-polar depression, low self-esteem, drug addictions and dysfunctional relationships. It took both of us decades to rid ourselves of the baggage imposed upon us through sexual abuse and the trauma of it. Personally, I can say that I have truly found the freedom God intends for all His children to walk in, and my sister did too, but only after years and years of struggle.

What I have discovered in my journey to wholeness is that freedom begins where shame ends. Freedom is the recognition of the root cause of our pain and the ability to respond to that pain differently than how we may have previously. Shame is the biggest barrier to finding peace and joy and will remain with us as long as we allow it to. It only ends when we examine it closely and bring it into the light, when we process it and uncover the truth of its origins. When we refuse to believe the lies it tells us, shame meets its end, and we are free to discover all God has for us.

Maybe you have endured similar sexual abuse trauma as a child, or maybe as an adult. Maybe you have been sexually assaulted or trafficked, or maybe you have walked through some other experience that has caused deep wounds and distress. Whatever the exact details of your trauma might be, chances are you understand all too well the weight of fear and shame I have described. They're not the only feelings trauma and abuse survivors have to process, but I believe they are the most debilitating. Shame, especially, robs you of your peace, your identity, your potential, and your purpose. If you are like most abuse survivors, you long for wholeness but you don't trust anyone enough to help you get there. The thought of being vulnerable or opening up to someone terrifies your soul. You want help, but it's just so hard to let down your guard long enough to receive it. I know, I have been there. I refused help for years. Please trust me when I say the uncomfortableness of asking for help, of digging deep and resolving your wounds is worth it! I hope you will pursue your healing sooner rather than later.

If you are reading this book and you have not experienced the burdens of fear and shame mentioned above, it is likely that you know someone who has. Approximately 1 in 5 women report having been sexually abused or assaulted at some point in their life, many in their childhood. Many more never report it at all. Can I encourage you to keep reading? Your understanding of this topic and your willingness to reach out to women who have walked through these difficulties could be the very thing they need to put them on the path to recovering their hope and discovering their own freedom.

My heart's deepest desire is to help those who are trapped by fear and shame to find freedom, identity, and purpose. As you read this book, my prayer for you is that you will also find hope and the courage to ask for the healing help you need. You may need assistance from a counselor, life coach or trusted ministry leader and that is okay.

This book will hopefully be a starting place for you. In its pages we will look at the difference between fear, authentic shame and false shame and the differences between healthy and unhealthy ways of dealing with them. We will examine a healthy framework for effectively dealing with these emotions. We will explore ways in which you can understand your true identity and examine how to learn what your unique purpose is in life.

To look beyond the damage to find healing we must first examine the nature of trauma, fear, and shame to deal with them in a restorative manner. The three are closely related and often intertwined with each other so it is important that we untangle them and understand their relationship to each other, as well as their individual traits. Understanding the role trauma, fear, and shame play in keeping us trapped in the past is the first step in learning to overcome them.

Unwrapping the layers of your trauma, fear and shame are likely to be as challenging as it was for me to be excited about opening that Christmas gift, if not more so. This journey will not be easy, but if you see it through it will be worth it. You will discover the truth of who God has created you to be. You will find that the fear and false shame that have held you in bondage for far too long no longer have power over you. On the other side of the struggle, you will discover who God created you to be and you will recognize the purpose you were intended to fulfill. You will have peace. You will experience joy. You will be free.

"It is for freedom that Christ has set us free. Stand firm, then, and do not let yourselves be burdened again by a yoke of slavery."

Galatians 5:1

Chapter One Journal Prompts:

In what ways have you started or attempted to begin your healing journey?

____

____

____

____

____

____

What do you hope life will look like for you when you have found your freedom, identity, and purpose?

____

____

____

____

____

____

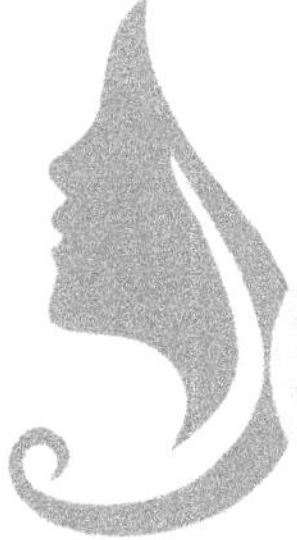

2.

The Aftermath of Abuse

Trauma

One afternoon I was sitting at my desk at work as a coworker was coming down off a ladder. Suddenly another co-worker shouted "earthquake." Thinking it was a joke, the one who had just stepped off the ladder replied, "ha-ha, very funny." You could tell by her voice that she was not amused. The problem was that it wasn't a joke. As I looked out the window, the trees in the fields across the street were swaying, so much so that they nearly laid over on their side. By the time I scrambled under my desk, the earthquake had subsided. The swaying ended as quickly as it began and the whole thing only lasted 15 seconds.

I worked in a retail environment for an independent retailer in Northern California, about 120 miles away from the epicenter of the 1989 Loma Prieta Earthquake, and yet we had felt the effects even at that distance. As immediate news reports unfolded, the earthquake measured 6.9 on the Richter scale and had done significant damage throughout the Bay Area. Thousands of structures, homes and businesses had been damaged. Most notably, a 1.25-mile-long section of the upper level of the Nimitz Freeway collapsed on the lower deck killing 42 people. The Bay Bridge also had a section of decking that collapsed causing one fatality. While the initial repairs of the Bay Bridge happened within a month, the longer process of complete retrofitting wasn't complete until 2014, 25 years later. The repairs to the Nimitz Freeway similarly took a great deal of time to complete, 12 years, but required significant rerouting after the demolition and cleanup of debris. The total cost of damages from the earthquake were estimated to be in the 5-to-6-billion-dollar range.

Just like an earthquake, trauma happens unexpectedly and quickly; the duration can be very short but extremely intense. Traumatic events can take just minutes, or even seconds to occur and sometimes they are over before we even realize what is going on, but the effects are far reaching and long lasting. They touch every part of our psyche and reshape the way we view ourselves in the world. The damage we personally experience also deeply impacts those closest to us, as well as our relationships with them. The trauma imposed by sexual abuse, assault and exploitation can cause great harm physically, emotionally, relationally, spiritually, and psychologically.

When trauma is repeated over a period of time, like abuse often is, it resembles aftershocks of an earthquake which can intensify and prolong the damage that has already been done. Under these circumstances, chronic trauma is inflicted. Being subjected to chronic trauma through ongoing abuse often causes women to experience a profound sense of helplessness, low self-esteem, feelings of worthlessness, fear, and shame. If you are a survivor of any kind of sexual trauma, you have probably experienced these things. What you may not realize though, is that what you are feeling is typical for what you have endured. While every survivor's response is unique to themselves, there are a great many commonalities within those responses. You are not alone.

Trauma has a long list of effects that include everything from physical illnesses to emotional disturbances, as well as stunted emotional development and neurobiological changes. If you are still struggling with any of these things, please consider getting counseling or coaching in addition to reading this book. While the list of traumatic responses is extensive, we will be dealing with the one that is most important to the mission of this manuscript in helping you to find your freedom, identity, and purpose: trauma's ability to affect the way one believes about themselves and their future.

Trauma can impose a great deal of doubt leading us to have limited expectations for living a typical life. Our vision for the future is often stunted by our experiences and we may have difficulty with fulfilling relationships, experiencing career growth that is rewarding, and recognizing beneficial opportunities. Our brains believe our felt internal monologues that we are not good enough, we are damaged, we are unworthy, which is why it is so important to deal with fear and shame. No matter how much someone else tells us we are loved and valued, we will have difficulty receiving it if we are telling ourselves the exact opposite. No matter how much someone tells us how talented and capable we are, we are not going to believe it if we think otherwise.

In the aftermath of trauma, these things are the emotional debris that must be managed. It is vital we understand and recognize how to examine our fear and shame-based emotions and beliefs in order to uncover the truth. The tearing down of these mindsets must occur before any repairs to our emotional wellbeing can be effective. And this repair process might only take a month to get us functioning in the world again, but very often, it will take years to completely restore our emotional health. Depending on the nature and damage of the trauma sustained, as well as the support systems in place, it could even take decades to find complete freedom from the debilitation caused by abuse. I hope and pray that you will be able to demolish and clear the debris of trauma quickly and embrace the process of being remade into who God created you to be. God did not cause your trauma. He loves you and wants to exchange those ashes of your past for all the beauty of life that He has for you.

Fear

The benches of the open-air amphitheater at Sugarloaf Ridge State Park were filled with campers that had come out for a night of entertainment. The evening was beautiful, cool, and crisp, as most nights in Northern California are. Some of the attendees would be part of the impromptu talent show and others would just watch. There were no elaborate sets or costumes, no time for lengthy rehearsals or the stress that comes with them, and no prizes to be won. Yet, they all came at the invitation of a six-year-old girl who had an idea, a six-year-old little girl who had no inhibitions about going from campsite to campsite inviting people to come participate in something spontaneous and fun.

Many years later, I often wondered what happened to that young girl, that part of myself which had embarked on such an adventure, full of hope and confidence that my little idea would work out. After having experienced abuse, I had become terrified of what people might think of me. I was too intimidated by life to step out and do anything. I was afraid I had nothing to offer. I longed to be free, just as I was when I was six. Unfortunately, fear had become the thief which stole my peace, my optimism, and my courage.

Fear robs us of our talents, abilities, and dreams, and it has the ability to completely paralyze us. There are some legitimate biological reasons this happens. Understanding those reasons is the first step in the journey of overcoming fear so let's start with a working definition of what fear is. Lexico Dictionary online[1] defines fear as "an unpleasant emotion caused by the belief that someone or something is dangerous, likely to cause pain, or a threat."

Fear is meant to be a biological warning system to help us stay safe. When we experience a traumatic situation that causes us to be afraid, the brain stores all the details of that event. It records what we could smell, see, hear, and feel as a means to warn us of potentially dangerous situations in the future. In the face of fearful circumstances, the brain's ability for rational processing is

---

bypassed and the natural instincts to avoid harm take over. This means of self-preservation has benefits in life-or-death situations, but what happens when chronic trauma breeds chronic fear?

In the case of sexual abuse and trauma, all those recorded details previously mentioned become cues, or reminders of the abuse that was endured and can trigger a fear reaction even when we are perfectly safe. This ongoing or repetitious fear affects our memory, the way our brains process information, and our reactivity to the world around us. Faced with chronic fear, we can become immobilized emotionally and spiritually. Without dealing with the effects of fear, we essentially become stuck in life.

Living in constant fear is quite detrimental to us. When we begin to become aware that we are unnecessarily living in fear, shame also often begins to take root in our lives. As this happens, fear and shame become intertwined around us. Our fear feeds our shame and likewise our shame fertilizes our fear. Left untended, this unhealthy cycle begins to entangle our minds. Let's take a closer look at the fear/shame cycle with the following case study. (Name and identifying details have been changed to protect the participant's privacy).

Susie grew up in a home with an abusive father. When she was nine, he began grooming her to cooperate with his inappropriate actions to fulfill his sexual desires. Her father led her to believe that these interactions were normal and that it was okay if she liked the way he touched her. Susie's body responded to physical stimulus the way God intended it to do within a normal, healthy relationship. While her father's actions sometimes made her feel uncomfortable, she complied with his requests thinking that if it felt good, it must be okay.

Years later, when the abuse was uncovered and she became aware that type of behavior was far from normal, she felt shame over the physical pleasure her body experienced. The shame she felt was so intense that she began to feel like there must be something wrong with her. This shame began to cultivate a profound fear within her that if other people knew all of what she experienced, they would be repulsed by her and reject her. Susie then began to believe that because she was so afraid for this to be discovered, it must be true that she was a repulsive person; and this belief only reinforced the shame she felt. Can you see how this cycle is perpetuated?

This case study is an unfortunate reality for many women who were sexually molested and abused at any age. As victims learn that these events of abuse are not typical, there is a tendency to feel responsible for things that are out of our control. This leads to a horrible cycle of fear and shame trapping us in the past. To better overcome this cycle, we must also take some time to more closely examine what shame is and how it affects our lives.

Shame

The overcast morning towards the end of winter somehow seemed fitting as I parked my car at city hall. Because my mom and sister needed to be there earlier, I arrived alone to give my testimony against my abuser. As I made my way to the building that housed the courtroom, I found the slightest bit of comfort in wearing my favorite purple cable knit sweater with a button collar. The buttons were square, and the collar turned down like one on a polo shirt would. I wore it with a pair of gray wool tweed slacks. I sometimes think it is strange that I remember those details so vividly when many other memories are a blur.

I also remember that my biological father had come to show support, but I could not bear to have him in the courtroom. How could I speak of those atrocities that had happened to me if he was sitting there? The slightest indication of any remorse, disgust, or disappointment he might have expressed would have made it impossible for me to say the things I knew needed to be said in order to confirm my abuser's guilt. In so many ways, I wished my dad hadn't learned about what I had been through. I longed for him to see me as the daughter I was before I had been abused. I felt so broken and damaged. More than I already feared that I was to blame, I feared that hearing the details would bring my dad to the same conclusion. The shame I felt was unbearable.

Shame is the painful emotion that causes us to experience humiliation, regret, remorse, distress and even self-loathing. Just like fear, shame has a legitimate function in our lives. It is meant to help us learn to overcome acting foolishly or making harmful choices. Legitimate shame is what is experienced when you have missed the mark knowing that you could have done better. It is the sorrow you feel when your actions have unjustly caused someone else pain, grief, or disappointment. Legitimate shame is born from true remorse of doing something wrong and invites you to be a better person and to act better going forward.

There's another side to shame though. It is the false and illegitimate emotion that beats us up and convinces us that our pain, grief, and disappointment are all our fault. It persuades us to believe that we are the responsible party for the things someone else has done to us or done to those we love. Illegitimate shame leads us to accept the idea that we are broken, worthless and undeserving and could never be anything else. Anger, rage, anxiety, loneliness, and emptiness also often accompany our shame and we are left imprisoned in these emotions.

This kind of shame keeps us from believing good things about ourselves and often prevents us from being able to receive love from others, especially the love of God our Father. It shapes the perception of our identity and keeps us from being all God created us to be. In his book Dream Big, Bob Goff says: "Shame has one goal and one goal alone: to keep you cemented in a dark past while it hides a beautiful future from you." Shame is a barrier keeping us from knowing who we truly are and living a life of peace and purpose. When we recognize these things about shame, we can begin the hard work of overcoming it and moving into the freedom of the beautiful life God has for us.

Chapter Two Journal Prompts:

In what ways have fear and shame kept you from your healing?

____

____

____

____

____

____

In what ways are you able to identify your shame as illegitimate?

____

____

____

____

____

____

3.

Overcoming the Shame

I could hear the sound of an electrical tool coming from the neighbor's backyard as I sat at the kitchen table looking out the window into my yard. It was a warmish winter day, and the grass was brown and dried out. Before long, the noise stopped and out of the corner of my eye, I saw the neighbor repeatedly picking up a large sheet of plywood and throwing it on the ground. My curiosity drew me closer to the window where I discovered the electrical metal grinder he had been using to take apart a metal storage building had sparked a fire in the dry grass.

Every time he picked up that piece of plywood and dropped it on top of the fire, he was fanning the flames out and spreading the fire which had begun moving towards my home. In my panic, I ran to the sink to fill a pot with water, but I had forgotten that the city had previously notified me that the water would be off for several hours that day. Sure enough, when I turned the faucet, nothing came out.

Mind racing, I moved back to the window so I could assess the situation and dialed 911 to report the fire. Of course, the dispatcher suggested I turn on the water and try to keep the fire contained. Right, why hadn't I thought of that idea? I was frustratedly trying to explain to her why that wasn't a good option when I looked out the window again and saw my above ground swimming pool. How did I miss that, the solution was right in front of me. Dropping the phone, I grabbed the stew pot, ran out to the pool, and started bailing water out and onto the fire. It was extinguished before the fire department even arrived.

In life, we are often presented with options as to how we can deal with a problem or a situation. Many times, we spring into action without giving a second thought about whether our approach will work, like my neighbor whose effort to smother the fire only made it spread. Other times, we know what we need to do but the resources aren't readily available to us, like my water having been shut off. In either case, we sometimes miss the answer that is staring us in the face, like my swimming pool, because it wasn't the solution we were looking for.

Overcoming fear and shame is often like this. In our pain and anxiety, we grasp at anything around us to try and find relief, often making the problem worse. Or we become hyper-focused on what we think will work only to discover we don't have the resources we need to move beyond our past. Sometimes we are presented with a tool bag of resources to help fix our condition, but when we pick up those tools, we often put them back down once we discover how heavy they are or how awkward they feel in our hands. Every once in a while, we get lucky, and we become aware of a solution we hadn't thought of, and it works out. From experience I can say that it is far better to learn how to use the tools and resources available to you than to wait to stumble upon a good solution.

To truly overcome the effects of our past experiences it takes courage, determination, and intentionality. To embrace the process of being remade, we must leave the familiarity of the known and move forward in the uncertainty of the unknown. That is often a difficult process but the freedom, identity and purpose that will be gained from it is worth it.

To be really intentional about finding our healing, we must identify the type and source of our shame. Are we experiencing a false shame? It is a shame that brings a sense of condemnation.

What we are feeling is condemnation when it comes from our own insecurities or other individuals who try to manipulate us. Condemnation makes us feel worthless. It is about who we are. It is the voice that says we have no value, and we never will so we should just give up. That is never God's message to us. This false shame is often the one we most need to resolve on our journey to wholeness.

Authentic shame is the type that serves a legitimate function in our lives, that of conviction. Conviction, while sometimes uncomfortable, is always meant to make us a better person and draw us nearer the heart of the Father. It is the knowledge that we have fallen short of how we have been called to live accompanied by the encouragement that God's grace is enough to redeem every legitimate mistake we make.

Regardless of the type of shame we experience, our default method of dealing with it and fear is often destructive, tearing us down and leading us deeper into its prison. We may hope that we will find the answer on our own but conquering our fear and shame is just too important to leave to chance. When we choose to be intentional about our healing, the process is much more likely to be reconstructive, leading us to the hope and wholeness we desire. By examining both ways of handling our pasts, we can determine where we are and how we got there in the process. When we can see the value of dealing with our pasts in a healthier manner, it helps us to make a more intentional choice.

It is important for us to note these differences between destructive and reconstructive methods of dealing with our shame, whether it is legitimate or illegitimate shame. But it is imperative that we, as survivors, know how to deal very specifically with the illegitimate version of shame. Therefore, we will take a look at both of these methods within the context of false shame as it is the biggest hindrance to becoming who God created us to be.

In the next chapter we will look at both the destructive and reconstructive coping methods of dealing with shame.

The Ineffective Way & The Better Way

Not long after I moved to Texas after growing up in Northern California, my cousin invited me to a rodeo the first weekend in June. Having only been in Texas a few weeks, I dressed for the event like I would for any evening event in my home state. I donned several layers of clothes because in my experience, no matter how hot the day might be, it always cooled down in the evening. So, with my jeans, boots, mock turtleneck, long sleeved button-up shirt on and a sweater in tow I headed out to the arena.

It was a hot day, and I was unbearably warm in all my layers at 6:00pm but I assumed that I would be comfortable enough in an hour or two. At 10:00pm I was still uncomfortably warm and asked my cousin "when is it going to cool down?" I thought she was joking when she responded with "October", so I rephrased my question: "No, when is it going to cool down tonight?" Much to my dismay she stated, "It's not."

When I got dressed that evening, I didn't know what I didn't know. Walking through the aftermath of sexual abuse and exploitation is similar. We don't grow up learning about how to heal from something that hasn't yet happened to us. There is so much to the healing process that we don't know before we get there and sometimes, we get it wrong, especially when trying to walk through it on our own.

I share this with you because as you read on, you may recognize the ways in which you have dealt with your abuse under the category of "the ineffective way." You didn't know what you didn't know. There is no shame in that so please do not pick up any more shame on your journey to freedom. We must become aware of and understand how shame has worked in our lives and how we have responded to it in order to be liberated from it.

The Ineffective Way

The ineffective way of dealing with fear and shame is quite destructive. It consists of four distinct components: define, defeat, defend, and deny. This method tends to be our default way of coping. It moves us further and further from who God created us to be and often cements us in living in our past. This is a terribly ineffective way to find lasting healing and hope.

When we default to a destructive means of dealing with shame, the first step is to allow ourselves to be defined by what we have experienced. We are deceived into believing that our past trauma, abuse, exploitation, and mistakes make us who we are. In this damaging mindset, we also allow ourselves to think that we do not deserve anything better.

It doesn't take long living as someone defined as worthless before we begin to operate from a mindset of defeat. Living defeated is what we do when we live believing there is no hope for recovery and healing from the trauma. Living life like we have been defeated and are without hope will also lead us into a life of depression and anxiety. Defeated living blinds us to truth and often allows Satan to trick us into living in a way that is the exact opposite of the life God intends for us to abide in.

Sexual abuse and exploitation survivors tend to respond to everything in the world around us through the lens of trauma, disappointment, self-blame, and hopelessness. As we deal with the false shame, we have allowed to define us, we tend to operate in defensiveness anytime we feel criticized or judged. We defend our outlook on life and our brokenness, as well as the reasons we can't move past it. It is here where we begin to believe the lies that we don't need anyone and that we can protect ourselves from being hurt again.

Finally, in our default efforts to manage the false shame we carry, we come to a place of denial. We mistakenly believe that if we deny it happened or minimize the impact of the trauma, we have experienced that we will be better. We fool ourselves into thinking that we will forget by burying all the hurt and pain and somehow that will make life better. By doing so, we live a defeated life, surrendering the hope of becoming something more than a victim. We resign ourselves to an existence of feeling isolated, alone, and hopeless.

These destructive ways of dealing with our fear and shame will never set us free. They are often shrouded in secrecy and silence which only serve to fertilize and feed the shame we feel even more. These destructive coping mechanisms will only tear us down and cause further damage to our emotions and spiritual well-being. We have only taken a look at them in order to recognize harmful methods of overcoming what we have endured.

If you recognize any of these things as a tactic you have used or defaulted to as a way to overcome, or even just to survive, please do not beat yourself up over your past coping mechanisms. You didn't know what you didn't know. I urge you to keep moving forward and keep reading. I believe you will come to understand there is a better way as you continue with this book.

The Better Way

In healthy homes, children's lives are being fashioned and constructed every day by the care and attention they get from loving family members. This construction of one's life is further built upon in meaningful social constructs like school and church. But abuse is destructive, tearing down and damaging the foundations that have been built. Abuse survivors are not starting with a clean slate and building something new, they are rummaging around in the debris for the good things that were buried or lost. Finding freedom is about reconstruction of what has been destroyed in a healthy way. Therefore, we will be discussing the better way a survivor can overcome their past as reconstructive.

Just as there are four components of the destructive method, there are four factors for dealing with false shame in a better way and a reconstructive manner: recognize, retrain, release, and refocus. I will outline these components now and later in the text we will examine how to apply each one of them to our lives so that we can walk in the identity, purpose and freedom God has for us.

Re-constructively dealing with the illegitimate shame we carry from abuse takes intentionality, vulnerability, and effort. The work involved may be intense, and seemingly more difficult than the destructive way we often tend to cope with things, BUT it is also the more rewarding way, bringing healing and wholeness. I challenge you not to shy away from the hard work of being remade. It is worth it.

Recognition is the first step we must take to re-constructively deal with the false shame we carry around. We recognize and acknowledge the truth of our experiences, our responses to our experiences, and our emotions concerning them. In our trauma response, we sometimes sweep things under the carpet trying to forget them, rather than dealing with them. The problem with this is you eventually trip over the mound of things you've pushed into a pile under the rug. Giving recognition to the facts of what you have endured does not validate those things in the sense of making them acceptable, it just allows you to see them factually.

Once we have given recognition to what we had previously tried to bury and hide, we begin to retrain our brains. This is the work of learning how to respond to the world around us rather than reacting to it through the lens of our trauma. Again, it requires effort. When something happens, you intentionally take time to process it so you can respond purposefully rather than reacting out of your woundings or emotions. We will take a closer look at the differences between reacting and responding in the following chapter.

As we learn to retrain ourselves in the way we deal with things, it prepares us for the next step: release. This is the process of surrendering our trauma, trauma responses and false shame to the Lord so they are no longer the driving forces in our lives. If your abuse was extensive, this may be a step you return to from time to time. I know in my own life, even when I feel like I have dealt with an issue, some underlying emotion or memory will bubble to the surface. It's important when you experience this to practice releasing whatever is coming to the surface back to the Lord.

Finally, after we have released what we need to let go of, we can begin the work of refocusing on the possibilities in front of us rather than the destruction of our pasts. We refocus on who we are becoming rather than dwelling on who we were in response to what we walked through. God longs for us to walk in the identity He intended for us to have, not the one created by the abuse we experienced at the hands of others. In the pages to come, you will find a more detailed process for each of these productive steps in dealing with shame re-constructively.

Chapter Three Journal Prompts:

How have you tried to deal with shame in the past? Have your methods been effective?

____

____

____

____

____

____

Which of the steps, if any, in The Better Way that you can immediately put into practice immediately?

____

____

____

____

____

____

Navigating the
Better Way

4.

Recognize

While growing up in California, the mountains were a very distinct part of the geography that my sense of direction was dependent upon. I knew if they were on my right I was headed north and if I was driving away from them towards the coast I was going west. I rarely needed a map because I knew the landscape.

When I moved to Texas though, there were no mountains. As far as I was concerned, it was entirely flat, and my sense of direction was lost. Using the landscape to navigate was no longer an option. I had to learn a new way to get around and use new methods to help me do so. Maps became a necessary tool for me to learn the unfamiliar landscape in which I had been replanted.

As we move from a default method of dealing with trauma to an intentional one, the unfamiliarity of the process may cause you to feel as if you have lost your sense of direction. This new way of dealing with our past may initially feel awkward and the tools introduced in these chapters may take some practice before they come easily to you. Don't lose hope! Embrace new methods of coping and find the tools you need to help you along the way. Let this chapter serve as a map as you take the next step towards a life of wholeness and healing.

Re-constructively dealing with our brokenness will also require us to allow ourselves to be vulnerable. We must allow ourselves the time and space we need to see our pasts and our reactions as they are. We must dig through the lies for the truth of what we have been through and how it has affected us. The amount of time and space needed will be different for everyone. Please do not feel the need to rush through the process. Much of this process happens in the first step of our intentional method of dealing with shame: recognize.

In this step of dealing with shame, we must honestly assess seven truths about our abusive experiences.

Truth #1 - Defining Sexual Abuse and Exploitation

Sexual abuse is any form of sexual behavior or contact a victim is unwillingly exposed to or coerced into by someone in a position of authority or perceived power. Sexual abuse becomes exploitation when the victim is subjected to perpetrators of abuse for the gain of another individual. Both abuse and exploitation are acts of violence no matter how cunningly they are committed by the abusers. Sexual abuse often occurs in childhood and within the context of incest.

Regardless of when sexual abuse or exploitation happens, to the degree it occurs, and who the perpetrator is, it is a horrific experience that infringes on basic human rights and dignity. It leaves a wake of damage that can take years or decades to overcome. Those who experience these things often have difficulty maintaining healthy relationships, feeling valued, and experiencing confidence and security. Even so, healing IS possible! Please do not let these facts discourage you from pressing in and becoming who you were created to be.

Truth #2 - There is Healing in Acknowledging

As long as we try to avoid the reality of our pasts, we will remain stuck and be unable to begin the work of overcoming what we have been through. To acknowledge something is to admit the existence or reality of our circumstances. Furthermore, it is admitting the truth about those situations or encounters that have harmed us.

Acknowledging that we have been taken advantage of against our will, by someone else, helps us to see that the actions of others are the cause of our wounds. It also lets us understand that we are not to blame. We mustn't try to rationalize what others have done. The abuse happened to us, at the hands of someone else, and it was wrong, it was hurtful, and damaging. Admitting the truth of our experiences can help us begin to understand why we feel the way we do about many other things. In turn, this will help us in working through the recovery process.

If you remember from our discussion about trauma earlier in the book, trauma takes time to recover from. While sexual abuse and trauma often follows a pattern, every person's experiences are unique to them. Therefore, the healing process is also unique. Some may recover more quickly than others, but we should avoid comparing our journey to that of someone else. Our walk to wholeness takes as long as it takes and that is okay. Recognizing this and giving yourself permission to take as much time as needed is important.

Truth #3 - You Could Not Have Prevented What Happened

If you were manipulated or coerced in any way concerning the abuse you suffered, give yourself grace. You didn't know what you didn't know, and you are not responsible for the theft of your innocence. If you remember our case study in the introduction, you are aware that many perpetrators go to great lengths to make their actions and the activities they engage in with their victims seem normal. In the case of childhood sexual abuse, you were most likely too young to know and understand the implications of the actions taken against you. Even if you experienced abuse or exploitation as a teenager or adult, you are likely to have been manipulated and taken advantage of, and the responsibility of such actions lies fully with the abuser.

If you were assaulted, know that it is nearly impossible to prevent the unexpected. In the presence of danger, the body's neurological response is for the brain to take over and initiate a fight, flight, or freeze course of action. This reaction overrides your will and your emotions. Your body goes into auto-pilot mode, which means that what happened to you was not your fault. It's worth repeating. . . what happened to you was not your fault!

None of us are capable of predicting the future. We can plan every detail out to ensure our safety and still be blindsided by the unpredictable actions of abusers. No matter what lengths you might possibly have gone to, you could not have prevented it so please set aside all of the what if questions you are tempted to ask yourself. You are not responsible for the harmful actions of others that were done to you.

Truth #4 - Your Emotions Have Legitimacy

Whatever you are feeling are your feelings. You do not need to defend them, nor do you need to explain them. You may not even fully understand all your emotions at this point either and there is nothing wrong with that. As you purposefully and intentionally examine your thoughts and feelings, they will begin to make sense to you. Additionally, you will be able to discern what is the root cause behind them. Doing so will empower you as you work to resolve your trauma.

It is not unusual for victims of sexual atrocities to experience a wide range of emotions in the aftermath of their abuse. Some of these may include shock, anger, unbelief, isolation, grief, anxiety, confusion, worry, relief, fear, loss of control, or hopelessness. This is unfortunately not an extensive list, and the important thing to recognize here is that there are a lot of emotional responses to trauma.

While all these emotions do have legitimacy and should be acknowledged, it is vital to the healing process that you don't get stuck in them. Take note of them: what prompts you to feel that way? Are there specific triggers that temporarily interrupt your ability to think rationally? What tools or resources do you have that can help you evaluate your emotions and how to cope with them at any given time?

Our human tendency is usually to default to unhelpful coping strategies. We often want to avoid the pain at any cost and resort to methods we believe will help us avoid the hurt and bring us some measure of comfort. The problem with this way of dealing with our feelings is that it actually delays our healing and masks the truth. Abstaining from negative coping mechanisms in response to your emotions is crucial to your healing process.

While a vast array of emotions we experience are to be expected, common negative coping skills include self-criticism, drug and alcohol use, avoidance, over-indulgence, obsessiveness, and behaving in an excessively controlling manner. These methods can all cause us setbacks in finding a way through the pain to the wholeness we desire. Acknowledge your emotions but look for healthy ways of managing them.

Truth #5 - Past Trauma Can Alter Our Present Perceptions

In a previous chapter, the effects of trauma were discussed briefly. It is important for us to recognize that our past trauma plays a role in our present perceptions until we become fully aware of what is happening in our brains. Actual physical changes to the function of both the amygdala and the hippocampus make it difficult for us to accurately discern that we are no longer in danger from our past experiences. These changes also often interfere with our cognitive ability, causing us to mistakenly identify harmless people and current circumstances as dangerous.

The brain stores the details of our negative experiences. The sights and sounds around us, the odors and aromas we smell, and any tactile sensations we encounter are all recorded by our subconscious. The memories of those things can be used as a warning system at a later date, even if no danger is actually present. It is not unusual for similar circumstances to trigger a flashback to the abuse we were subject to. Another survivor I know shared that those of us who were abused do not remember our abuse, we relive it. Which is why in the face of even perceived danger our brains override our reasoning and critical thinking skills.

Without an awareness of these changes, we will continue to react to the world through the lens of trauma. But by recognizing our propensity to see the world in a skewed manner, it becomes easier to work on healing the brain and changing how we interact with the world around us. Awareness enables us to ask ourselves questions that will help us engage our critical thinking skills. When we can think critically about our current situation we are empowered to move beyond the trauma responses that resulted from our abuse.

Truth #6 - It's Not God's Fault Either

I remember being extremely angry at God for allowing the abuse that occurred in mine and my sister's lives. It took me almost two decades to realize that my abuse was not God's fault. Maybe you are one that has been angry, or is still angry, with God for what you have experienced. It is not an uncommon reaction. I am hoping though that you are willing to open yourself to the possibility that our all-knowing and all-powerful God is deeply grieved by the abuse you have experienced.

You see God loved us so much from the very beginning of creation that He gave each and every one of us a free will. We get to choose how we live our lives, whether or not we believe in Him or serve Him. And He doesn't have favorites, well maybe Jesus is His favorite. Even if that is true, God does not show favoritism. Jesus was not spared the torture leading up to His crucifixion nor was He spared a painful death. He experienced hate and abuse at the hands of others because God does not impose on the gift of free will He has given us.

What He does do when we live a life surrendered to Him is promise to redeem the trials and challenges that touch our life and turn them around for our good and His glory. God hates that you have been hurt and longs to bring you healing and hope. He deeply desires to restore you to your true identity in Him and to the plan and purpose He has for your life. "And the God of all grace, who called you to his eternal glory in Christ, after you have suffered a little while, will himself restore you and make you strong, firm and steadfast." 1 Peter 5:10

Once we have given recognition to each of these truths and can understand the power and the value behind acknowledging them, it's time for us to take the next step and intentionally retrain ourselves to respond to our circumstances in a way that moves us forward.

Chapter Four Journal Prompts:

Which of these six truths is most difficult for you to accept and why?

____

____

____

____

____

____

Which of these truths brings you the most comfort? Explain why you think that is.

____

____

____

____

____

5.

Retrain

I went to college late in life. I had always been a good student growing up and learning had always come easy to me. Just a week into my English class our professor gave us a pop quiz on our reading assignments. Much to my surprise and dismay, I could not recall a single thing I had read. I hadn't retained any of it and my first grade on a college assignment was an F. I had a choice at that moment to react to the situation by feeling sorry for myself and giving up or to respond to it by embracing the fact that I needed to relearn how to learn.

Abuse and trauma can create in us this system of reacting to people and events rather than responding to them. The difference between reacting and responding is what drives our need to retrain the way we think.

Reacting to something occurs when we allow our emotions and impulses to drive the way we interact with what is happening. It is a quick and hasty process that involves very little thought and very little control. On the other hand, responding to something happens when we allow our knowledge and expertise to guide us in our interactions. It often requires a pause in action and involves thought on our part. Responding is the more metered and disciplined way of relating to the world around us.

Interestingly enough, when the fight, flight, or freeze process is triggered in our brains, it takes at least 20 minutes after the stressors are removed for our adrenaline to subside. Once it has, we are able to think more clearly, helping us to regain our calm. The goal of retraining our brain is to empower ourselves with knowledge to view the world in a healthy way, allowing us to operate within our communities genuinely and authentically. When we accomplish this, we can begin to live out the life of purpose and meaning God has for us.

So, how do we retrain our brains? Let's look at three strategies to help us move from being reactors to responders.

#1 Practice Awareness

When you begin to become upset, take inventory of your circumstances and your emotions: What is happening? How are you feeling? Why are you feeling that way? If you are unable to quickly put the answers to any of these questions into words, know that you would benefit from a time out. If someone else is involved, politely explain that you need to take a break from the conversation. Then, when you are able, take time to contemplate what was driving your emotions. Remember, it takes the brain at least 20 minutes to recover from flight, fright or freeze mode so do not feel pressured to rush the process.

As you are evaluating the situation, what are you feeling? Are those feeling genuinely about the current circumstances or has what happened dredged up something from the past? Journaling your thoughts and responses to these questions could be very beneficial in helping process your emotions and increasing your awareness. If you discover that particular things trigger a reactionary response in you, this knowledge helps increase your awareness. The next time you begin to feel upset about something similar, it will be easier to recognize the source of your agitation and you will be better equipped to pause and respond rather than react.

Become aware of what your default ways of addressing your frustrations and emotions are. Dealing with your feelings and triggers is what is important in this process. What we want to avoid is sweeping emotional events under the carpet and avoiding them. This method of coping only masks the problem. While you consciously choose to ignore what is going on, your subconscious is keeping track of everything that needs resolving. Just as adding to the pile under the carpet will cause a physical tripping hazard, ignoring your thoughts and feelings can cause you to be emotionally tripped up, leading you into a reactionary response. When this happens, it may ultimately cause further damage or delay your healing journey.

#2 Positively Pause

While taking a time-out was mentioned as a part of our first strategy in retraining the brain, we must be very purposeful in the activities we engage in as we pause. Giving full vent to all our emotions in a time out can be just as counterproductive as allowing them to drive us in the heat of the moment. Therefore, finding a purposeful and positive activity to engage in during our pause, or time out, is a crucial part of releasing our stress and retraining the brain.

To positively pause, you can engage in a wide variety of activities, anything from physical to artistic to thoughtful. Think about the things that help you feel refreshed and reduce stress in your life. Also think about a variety of activities that can be employed in varying situations. You may only have time to go for a walk around the block or for a phone call to a friend you can trust to be objective but try to get the 20-minute break that is needed to recover from the flight, fight, or freeze response you have experienced. When you have more flexibility in your schedule, make time to go to the gym for a full work out or sit and do something creative. When we engage in purposeful activities that positively affect our mindset, we become equipped to respond to situations in constructive ways.

I encourage you to make yourself a list of the types of things you find enjoyable, relaxing, and even productive. Decide ahead of time which ones you will implement when needed. You may determine that different circumstances require different soothing tactics. Make a note of the types of things that cause you to need to positively pause and then mentally connect an activity to circumstances. The act of planning ahead for those heat of the moment events will help you be more successful in coping with them in a healthy way.

#3 Focus on Solutions

As we practice awareness and positively pausing, we must also focus on finding solutions. Allowing ourselves to rehearse the problem often leads to the exaggeration of its importance and a reigniting of our propensity to react negatively to the situation. This leads to keeping our thinking trapped in the emotional part of the brain. Yes, we must think about the problem, but we should do our best to separate the problem from our emotions so that we can find a means of dealing with difficult situations.

Focusing on preferred outcomes helps us to regain control of our actions, moving our thought processes from that emotional part of the brain to the rational or problem-solving area of it. And when you find a solution to the problem, your brain experiences a positive biological response which neurologically encourages you to focus on solutions more often.

When focusing on finding a solution, there are a few things to keep in mind: What does a successful resolution look like to you? Do you have the emotional resources you need to achieve the outcome you are hoping for, or do you need to seek assistance from a trusted friend, counselor, mentor or pastor? What is your role in the solution? What are your expectations from others? And what do you do when there seems to be no good solution, or someone is unwilling to participate in the solution you have come up with?

Thinking these things through and purposefully making these decisions ahead of time will go a long way in helping you retrain the way you interact with the world.

Retraining the brain will take practice. Do not beat yourself up for the times that you may still react rather than respond. When you do unintentionally react to a situation, take a step back and evaluate what you could have done differently. You may find that it is helpful to write out your plan so you can refer to it as needed. This will allow you to assess what worked and what did not. This will also help you to make a better plan and a better choice the next time you face a similar circumstance.

In the end, the important thing is to focus on your progress. The more you use these strategies, the more ingrained they will become. You will become more likely to respond in a healthy way rather than reacting in a negative manner.

Chapter Five Journal Prompts:

After reading chapter five, how do you plan to tackle retraining your brain?

____

____

____

____

____

____

What specific activities can you personally engage in when you need to positively pause, practice awareness, or focus on solutions?

____

____

____

____

____

____

6.

Release

In 2015 my abuser passed away. I didn't really have any feelings about it until other people started to say things like "this world is a better place without him," "good riddance," and even "I hope he rots in hell." My sister had been hanging onto the hope that her father would one day admit to the harmful things he had done to us and apologize. Her heart longed for restoration and my heart hurt for her loss of hope for a renewed relationship. The only way forward for my sister was for her to choose to release her expectations and grieve the loss she was going through.

I don't think it is unnatural for us to want those who hurt us to acknowledge their crimes and apologize. And depending on the relationship between the abuser and the abused, I don't think that healing and reconciliation for the relationship are completely out of the question either. However, I do not believe that kind of reconciliation happens often. Any attempts at this type of restoration should be handled with extreme care and the assistance of a counselor or pastor.

Once we have acknowledged the truths about our past and have learned some tactics for retraining our brains, it is time for us to begin to release the past. It may have been the reality we lived for quite some time, but we do not need to continue living as though our future is dependent on those experiences. We must intentionally engage in the act of freeing ourselves from being held captive by the memories of what we endured and the habits that were created in us through our trauma.

The benefit of practicing release is that in doing so we allow ourselves to embrace our identity as a survivor rather than to continue living as a victim. The difference between the two is that a victim allows themselves to be defined by the trauma inflicted upon them whereas a survivor is someone who has walked through the recovery process and denies the past control over their future. They recognize that what has happened to them is just a part of their story; it is not their identity.

Practicing release is what empowers us to move from victim to survivor. The process is rarely an easy one and never happens by accident. We must intentionally choose to let go of the abusive influence of what we have endured. The steps to this process include what was outlined in both of the previous chapters, but the most impactful step, and probably the most difficult one on the road to release, is extending forgiveness.

Extend Forgiveness

According to an article from Greater Good Magazine, "Psychologists generally define forgiveness as a conscious, deliberate decision to release feelings of resentment or vengeance toward a person or group who has harmed you, regardless of whether they actually deserve your forgiveness."[2] Let's be clear, when we extend forgiveness, we are not defending or excusing the behavior of our abusers. An extension of forgiveness is not a discharge of guilt. It is an act of will, choosing to give importance to

----

2

https://greatergood.berkeley.edu/topic/forgiveness/definition accessed 12/15/22 your future health and well-being rather than giving power to your past.

There is purpose behind the directions God gives us to be forgiving. Colossians 3:13 states: "Bear with each other and forgive one another if any of you has a grievance against someone. Forgive as the Lord forgave you." And although the Bible doesn't expound upon the mental and emotional harm of unforgiveness, science does tell us that unforgiveness exacerbates our emotional distress by increasing our insecurities and fear, and by causing anxiety and depression.

Making strides in releasing our past through forgiveness may also be complicated by who you need to extend forgiveness to. Rarely is the abuser the only one we have felt wronged by. Often there is another party who failed to protect us, enabled the abuser, or refused to believe our cries for help. And sometimes, we even need to forgive ourselves for the self-blame and the false shame we have undeservingly accepted.

Forgiveness is a process too. If it is something you have struggled with being able to do, I understand. My own path to forgiveness was challenging and complicated. There were many times I had to readdress something I thought I had forgiven. There will be times as you process your trauma that you uncover things you've forgotten about or haven't quite resolved.

Forgiveness isn't always a linear activity. Occasionally, you will have to circle back and walk through the steps again. Each time you do, you will experience a bit more healing. Think of it like climbing a spiral staircase. Your steps may bring you back around to the same vertical point, but you have gained altitude. You are making progress even when it feels like you're in the same spot. Be encouraged by your advances no matter how small they may seem.

For now, I realize that asking you to forgive those who have caused you harm may be the single most difficult thing in this book that I recommend you do. But I promise you, it is also the single most important thing you can do on your journey to your freedom, identity and purpose.

Trust In God

Previously, in the recognition portion of overcoming shame we acknowledged the truth that what happened to us was not our fault, nor was it God's fault. In order to move forward in the process of releasing our past, we need to learn how to trust God. The definition of trust is "firm belief in the reliability, truth, ability, or strength of someone or something."[3] Trust, like so many other things on the journey to healing, requires us to make a deliberate choice to place our faith in someone or something. When we believe that God is able to love, care for, and heal us in every circumstance, we are trusting Him.

What does it take to develop an unwavering trust in someone? It usually involves getting to know them over a period of time. The best thing we can do to grow and nurture our faith and trust in the Lord is to spend time with Him. We will take a closer look at the practice of prayer in a later chapter but for now know that reading the Bible and developing the discipline of prayer are foundational to building a relationship based on trust.

At this point, I imagine that some of you reading this are thinking "Trust God? Where was he while I was being abused?" Can I share with you some insights from scripture? Let's look at Exodus 3:16-17. God is speaking to His people who have been held captive in slavery for generations. This is what He says "...I have watched over you and have seen what has been done to you in Egypt. And I have promised to bring you up out of your misery...." As I said before, God sees you, He knows you and every hurt you have been subjected to. Not only that, but He has a plan to deliver you from the pain of your past.

God wants to bring you out of all the heartache and destruction you experienced. But you must trust Him and release it all back to Him. There is nothing that has touched your life that He cannot turn around for your good. You might wonder why He would want to; because He loves you and because He loves others who are going

---

[3] *Trust* **Google Link accessed 4/7/23**

through what you have experienced. The Lord wants to bring you through to your complete healing so that you can live the life He created you to live. One full of love, passion, hopes, dreams, freedom, and purpose. Putting our faith in the Lord brings peace, strength, and confidence. Isaiah 26:3 tells us that He "will keep in perfect peace those whose minds are steadfast because they trust in [Him]."

Learning to trust God may take you some time. It will also require a purposeful effort on your part. Consider joining a Christian support group or Bible Study, learn how to put the spiritual discipline of prayer into practice, or asking your pastor if there is a mentor who can help you learn about the faithfulness of Jesus. There are survivors who are ready to take your hand and walk through this challenge with you. And if you can't find someone, call me. I would be honored to be a part of your healing journey.

Share Your Story

Leaning on others and sharing your story is also a crucial component to releasing the past. There is power in sharing your story! It is part of the restorative process to communicate with others what you have experienced. While your wounds are fresh or painful, seek out only trusted friends or professionals that can help you through the process. It is not a sign of weakness to talk with a mentor, life coach, pastor, counselor, or trusted friend. Doing so requires courage and determination. It won't be easy, and it may not happen quickly, but it will be worth it!

Feeling overwhelmed at the thought of being vulnerable is understandable. Don't think that you have to tell your entire story all at once. It will be both easier and more constructive to reveal your experiences in manageable chunks when you take the time to jot it down. This will also help you to clarify and organize your memories and thoughts to effectively deal with the emotions attached to them.

If sharing your story is a new experience for you that causes anxiety, try writing down exactly what you want to share. You can then edit it until you are comfortable with the way your story is phrased. Once you feel you have the appropriate words composed, you can choose to read them to the person you are sharing with. Your emotions will be projected through your voice and body language which will help the listener understand the message you are trying to convey.

To help you feel more relaxed with divulging difficult things to others, you should also choose the time and place. Select somewhere you feel comfortable and safe. You'll also want to pick a day, or time of day when you have plenty of time and are least likely to feel stressed or anxious. It will be easier to share if you are not feeling rushed, upset, or distracted by some other situation.

You may even want to prepare before sharing with someone. Think about exactly what you want to tell them and the feelings that will come up as you do. If you become anxious about the conversation you'll be having, go back to the retraining steps in the previous section. Practice those exercises until you are ready to have a discussion about your experiences. You get to set the pace and the tone of your healing journey. The quality of the healing you experience is more important than how quickly you achieve it.

I wish that I had heeded this advice sooner rather than later and received my healing earlier BUT it is never too late to begin! Once you have become comfortable talking through your story with those you trust, you may want to reach out to others who have had similar experiences. I have found so much insight and encouragement in sharing my story with others who can relate. Sometimes, those women are ahead of me in the healing process and sometimes they haven't come quite as far as I have, but either way I have found those conversations to be incredibly valuable.

One day, I hope you will be able to talk about your past openly and freely. It is so cathartic to be able to help open the eyes of those around us to the prevalence of abuse. When we bring awareness to others in our communities, we help in making the world a safer and better place. If the awareness that comes from sharing our stories prevents others from having a similar experience, then our past, our fears and our felt shame all lose their grip on us.

Chapter Six Journal Prompts:

What can you do to help you identify yourself as a survivor rather than a victim?

Which step in this chapter do you think will best enable you to move forward in your journey at this time?

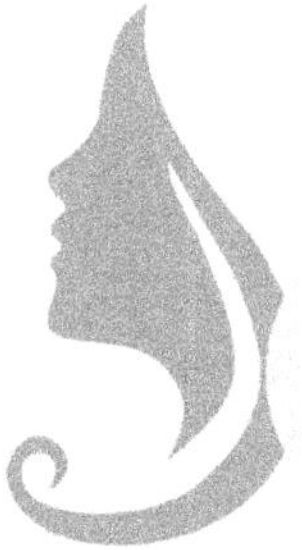

7.

Refocus

There was a time in my adult life when someone I cared for and trusted deeply hurt me. I was beyond angry at them. In my anguish over the situation, the Lord got ahold of this individual and they were genuinely repentant. Their relationship with God began to grow and flourish while I was left in the distress of my wounds.

One Sunday morning, I was feeling particularly sorry for myself and somewhat frustrated with God about the situation. In my angst, I asked Him why I had to suffer for this person's life to be so radically changed. A whisper in the back of my mind responded, "Why did my Son have to die on the cross for you?" Suddenly I felt convicted and refocused on not what someone else had done to me, but what God had done for me through the death of His son Jesus.

The refocusing step is a continuation of the release process. It is not ignoring what happened. It's the last step coming only after we have evaluated the actions that caused our trauma, after we have developed a healthier way to think, and after we have released ourselves from the damage. Refocusing is turning our attention away from the past, that can only trap us, and towards the future that can set us free.

As we determine that we will not allow our difficult history to hold us prisoner we set our sights on hope, healing, and possibilities. All those things can be a reality for us. However, refocusing on our potential may not produce immediate results. In fact, the outcomes will probably come gradually and that's okay.

Adjusting our focus will also probably be something we need to redo from time to time. I still find a need to do this occasionally. I have been walking out my healing for quite a while. I know it's sometimes hard to imagine that we have a future that is bright and full of promise, but the Bible encourages us that with the right focus a life of freedom, wholeness, and potential are possible. "Brothers and sisters, I do not consider myself yet to have taken hold of it. But one thing I do: Forgetting what is behind and straining toward what is ahead, I press on toward the goal to win the prize for which God has called me heavenward in Christ Jesus." Philippians 3:13-14

In order to press forward, there are several things we can do to refocus our thoughts on the future. We can practice awareness, begin building good habits, set some goals and manage our expectations.

Awareness

Have you ever found yourself going through your day on autopilot? You might be physically engaged in one activity, like driving or doing the dishes, but your thoughts are elsewhere. You're not paying any attention to what is going on at the moment. I don't know how many times I have missed where I was supposed to turn because my brain was not engaged with what I was doing. Once I miss my turn, I usually realize what I've done and refocus my attention on what I am doing.

One method of refocusing is to be aware of our thinking or what we are doing. Being aware is simply practicing recognition of our thoughts, actions, and emotions. When we begin to realize that our thoughts are drifting backwards, we must stop those thoughts in their tracks and replace them with the truth of what we are working towards. Losing sight of where we are going often results in finding ourselves somewhere we don't need to be. When we find our thoughts reverting to our old ways of thinking, we must remind ourselves that we are no longer victims, but we are overcomers.

Sometimes the past tries to sneak back into our present thoughts. I find that if I am beginning to feel anxious or stressed about something, it is a good practice to stop and ask myself what's at the root of those feelings. By being aware of thoughts that are causing stress and anxiety, I can evaluate why they are doing so. Then I can discern if those thoughts are something I need to discard or deal with. Awareness of your own thought processes may take some practice but the benefits of being able to refocus on the here and now are well worth the effort.

Don't be afraid to ask yourself what you are feeling, why you are feeling that way and what is causing those thoughts and feelings. Journaling your answers to these questions can bring valuable insight. Seeing your questions and answers on paper gives you the opportunity to evaluate them to determine if there is any truth in them or not. If we never discern the answers to those questions or the truthfulness of our answers, we will never be able to truly refocus on the healing that lies ahead of us.

Habit Building

Habits are actions or routines that become ingrained in our lifestyle. We can also learn to refocus by creating or identifying healthy habits and coping mechanisms. I am a very creative person so writing, crafting, and painting are some of the productive strategies I use to manage overwhelm and stress. Identify activities that you enjoy doing and that help you feel better when stress threatens to steal your peace.

Perhaps you enjoy cooking, running, hiking, long walks on the beach, a drive in the country, playing board games with friends, listening to worship music, or gardening. You can build new beneficial habits by adding something to one of your existing activities. For instance, if you enjoy listening to music, you can put on a set of headphones and listen to your favorite tunes while taking a walk. In this way you're connecting a new helpful activity to something that is already enjoyable for you.

Habits can take time to build so be patient with yourself. Consistently practice the new activity you want to develop until it becomes natural to you. Some people find they are more successful when they use a habit tracking system. Others may discover it is helpful to find someone who can assist them with accountability as they try to establish new routines. Find methods of habit building and follow through that work for you.

Finally, whatever healthy activities bring you a sense of peace and calm, engage in those often. Not only can they help you bring life back into a clearer focus when things are difficult, they can help maintain a healthy focus. Often this prevents one's stress and overwhelm from becoming a problem to begin with.

Goal Setting

One of the most productive ways of refocusing and turning your attention from dwelling on the past to looking to the future is setting goals for yourself. The goals you choose for yourself should be meaningful and manageable for you. You decide what you want to work towards and how you want to measure your success.

For example, consider that you set a goal for yourself of choosing healthy coping mechanisms when you begin to feel agitated. While this is a great target to aim for, how will you know when you are becoming successful at doing so? You might consider being more specific by including a measurement within the goal. For instance, your new one might look like this: When I begin to feel agitated, I will choose healthy coping mechanisms 7 out of 10 times. If you are currently never choosing healthy ways of coping, this could be a stretch for you so you might want to change the number. Honestly assess where you are currently and adjust your goal accordingly. Don't make it so easy that it doesn't stretch and grow you, but also don't make it so challenging that it discourages you and adds to your stress.

Additionally, when thinking about goals, you should determine how you will accomplish your objective. Perhaps when you get stressed and upset, you forget what healthier coping mechanisms are available to you. You will be better prepared for achieving your aim if you have tools and resources handy. You may write this more specific goal out as: When I feel stressed and agitated, I will go for a walk, journal my thoughts, or call a trusted friend. I will know I am making progress towards this when I can do it 7 out of 10 times. When your goals and plan for achieving them are written down, it is easier for you to learn what is working and what is not. If a particular goal or process is not helping you to refocus, consider scrapping it and trying something different.

The best goals you can plan and personalize for yourself are:

- Keep moving forward. - Ask yourself what this looks like for you. Your timeline for progress will be different than it will for others and there is nothing wrong with that. Also give yourself grace and know your capabilities. Allowing your pace to be determined by your limits is wisdom. Let wisdom determine your priorities as you seek your healing. It will help you to focus on what is most important. The most essential thing is to continue to move forward. Even one tiny step forward at any given time is progress. Write down a strategy to keep yourself on track for when you get stuck or take a step backwards and review it from time to time.
- Ask for help when needed. - Identify who your trusted sources are that you can turn to when you need assistance. It may be different people for different circumstances. Ask them if you can reach out to them occasionally for their assistance.
- Trust God in the process. - Remember, you are loved. God can and will redeem what you have been through. He has a place of wholeness, healing, and freedom for you. I know it's not always easy, but I promise, IT IS WORTH IT!

There are many resources available in print and online to help you with goal setting but if you struggle with this task, seek assistance from a trusted source or life coach. Remember, goal setting is an important tool in learning how to refocus and move forward.

Managing Expectations

As you refocus from the past to the present and future through the exercise of setting goals, it is important to manage your expectations. As mentioned before, this is a journey, it is going to take time. Setting realistic goals for ourselves through this process can help to keep you moving forward. You shouldn't expect that damage from abuse which occurred over weeks or years, or even minutes or hours, will disappear overnight. Complete restoration is not likely to be easily achieved so give yourself grace when it's hard, when it takes longer than expected, when you take a step or two backwards, and when you run into the unexpected along the way.

Setbacks will almost assuredly happen while you are on your journey to freedom. The unexpected will happen, you'll miss the goal you set for yourself, and sometimes you'll be triggered by something you thought you had already successfully overcome. While these bumps in the road can be disheartening, there are several things you can do to manage your expectations so that you don't get stuck along the way.

First, take time to reflect on what may have caused you to stumble. Take note of the specifics and ask yourself what you can do better the next time. Make a plan for how to do so. Journal your thoughts about the experience or talk it through with a friend who can encourage you.

Second, grieve if needed. We are really good at burying our feelings and even better at minimizing them when they are brought to the surface. Acknowledging how we feel about our experiences is allowed whether the feeling is rage, remorse, bitterness, shock, or any other number of emotions we might have. Hold those sentiments to the light and examine the truth behind them. No matter how valid our feelings are, they are simply like the warning lights on a car dashboard. They give us an indication that there is something wrong, but they don't necessarily diagnose or fix the issue. Sometimes we have to uncover the source of our emotions to deal with them and grieve our losses.

Third, don't get stuck in negative emotions and don't beat yourself up about having them. Give yourself grace and refrain from self-criticism. Be mindful of your capacity because none of us can deal with any one thing effectively if we're trying to deal with everything all at once. Our aim is to complete our healing journey, which happens one step at a time, as we learn to change the way we think.

Fourth, revisit any of the previous steps that you need to: Recognize, Retrain and/or Release to help you adjust future goals and expectations. Examine your objectives and determine what changes you might need to make.

Fifth, practice the positive coping skills you've identified for yourself. What is going to help you move forward again? Who can call to give you guidance? Which of your coping skills is most applicable and sustainable for the current season you are in or the circumstance you are facing?

Take care of yourself; sleep, water, healthy foods, and exercise are basic needs for everyone. But if it is a challenge to be successful in doing all of these, focus on getting plenty of rest. Even on our best days life is going to feel heavy and more challenging if we are tired or exhausted. Take care of yourself.

By recognizing and acknowledging the truth of all we've been through, retraining our brain to deal with our trauma in a reconstructive manner, releasing what we never could and never will be able to control or change, and by refocusing on the potential and possibilities of the future, we can be victorious over the strongholds of shame. Remember, where shame ends, freedom begins.

Chapter Seven Journal Prompts:

How do you think refocusing will be helpful to you in your healing journey?

Who can you ask to help you when your focus gets stuck on unhelpful things? You may list a few people for different circumstances.

Identity

8.

Introduction to Identity

I don't know about you, but one of the biggest aspects of who I had become after two years of abuse was fear. It owned me. Fear impacted every decision I made and every choice I failed to make. It was a stumbling block to any success I tried to achieve, and I longed to be free from it.

I love this quote from Ralph Ellison: "When I discover who I am, I'll be free." I kept hanging my hopes of walking in freedom on the next big event in my life. I thought I would discover who I really was when I turned 16, then 18, then 21. After that I dreamed of finding my identity as a wife, as a mother and even as a ministry leader. But the fear persisted, and I thought I would never escape from it.

Merriam Webster's online dictionary defines freedom as "the state of not being imprisoned or enslaved." For the purposes of this book, I define freedom as no longer being held captive by the trauma, fear, and shame of an abusive past.

Freedom begins with discovering who we are, the good and the not so good. There is liberty in recognizing we are a work in progress and in trusting that what God has to say about us is true.

We can walk in the identity we were created to have despite our past experiences, mistakes, and failures.

Identity Components

Worth noting is the fact that there are several components commonly identified by psychology that make up our identity. These are our self-concept, self-confidence, our values, as well as our natural giftings and personality traits. Let's take a closer look at these things to help us understand how our identity is typically developed.

Self-concept

Inwardly our identity is composed of our self-concept or who we perceive ourselves to be in relation to the people around us, including our roles as we interact with them. Self-concept develops throughout childhood and into adolescence based on our thoughts and feelings about ourselves. It can also be formed by our interpretation of how other people respond to us. Having a healthy self-concept requires a degree of self-awareness which allows us to examine why we think the things we do.

Self-awareness also enables us to know where the thoughts and feelings we have about ourselves are rooted. Did they form under a positive context or through abusive experiences? If self-concept was formed primarily through an abusive context, the likelihood that typical emotional development was stunted at the time of trauma is high. The good news is, with a little time and effort, we can change the way we think about ourselves. The steps outlined in chapter 5 on retraining our minds can be useful in guiding you to learn how to think differently about yourself and your circumstances.

Self-confidence

Outwardly, our identity takes shape as self-confidence. Our self-confidence levels impact the way we actually interact with others. If our self confidence is high, it is because we tend to believe positively about ourselves and are less likely to believe the negative criticisms of others about who we are. A healthy self-confidence is driven by a sense of significance and purpose.

Alternatively, low self-confidence forms when we believe the worst about ourselves. This can lead to a constant seeking of validation from other individuals and is often driven by the fear of failure or being seen as insignificant. When our self-confidence is unhealthy, we frequently take things too personally and worry too much about what others think of us.

Values

At the core of who we are we discover our values, or the things that are deeply meaningful and important to us. Values are the ideas and beliefs we deem most meaningful to who we are. They are the dividing line between activities and attitudes we will and will not participate in. These ideals typically guide our actions, choices, and decisions, thereby defining our personal character. For example, abuse survivors tend to value safety, honesty, understanding and compassion. These are the principles of what we hold dear and the ones we allow to guide our lives.

Values are formed through family experiences, the education system, community, culture, and society. For those who endured repetitive childhood abuse, it is possible for unhealthy values to have been formed. These unhealthy values reveal themselves as bad habits like lying, being manipulative, over-indulgent, and attention-seeking to name a few.

I encourage you to make a list of what is important to you, as well as one for how you spend your time, attention, and money. Write them down and compare them to one another to help you determine any changes you need to make. Be open to the idea that what you think is important may not actually be as significant to you as you thought. Anything you give your time and attention to or spend your money on are actually the things you value. If you find that you are unhappy with what you have developed as values in your life, remember, every day is a new day and a new opportunity to allow God to do a new thing in your life. Ask Him for the direction you need to adjust your habits in a way that aligns with what is truly valuable.

Traits, Talents & Skills

And of course, we can't talk about who we are without giving consideration to our unique personality traits, talents and skills. All these things are the distinctive attributes, features and qualities of our identity. Personality traits are the enduring personal characteristics by which we are often known. We can be open with others or guarded in what we share. Some of us are very outgoing while some are shy. There are adventurers and those who play it safe and there are people who handle life with a pleasant grace while others are harsh and overly direct.

The talents we have come from the ability to excel at certain tasks. My mother excelled in mathematics, making her an excellent insurance adjuster while I am not naturally good with numbers, but I am very creative. You may be very athletic, artistic, good with words, or any other number of things. Talents are typically those things that come very naturally to us, but they can also be improved on.

While skills may be things we are talented in, they are more accurately something we have worked at to learn. Someone who is naturally creative, may work to learn how to use their creativity by developing the skill of painting or cooking or building. Someone talented with mathematics, like my mother was, may learn how to teach math or how to be an accountant. Skills are the result of what we learn to do with the traits and talents we have.

These three aspects of our identity, traits, talents, and skills are the outward expression of identity where our self-concept, self-confidence and values are more representative of our identity inwardly. These expressions of our identity are all about us, our experiences, our development, our natural abilities, and interests. However, there is one more aspect of identity I would like for us to take a look at that primarily affects us from without: labels.

Labels

In addition to these identity components, there are so many voices in this world, including our own, trying to dictate to us where and how to find our identity. We are bombarded every day with information from the world about who we should be. Every television show we watch, every commercial we see, and every social media post we look at sends us messages of how we should think or act in society. Our teachers, parents, peers, and even our abusers, try to influence who we are by labeling us. Sometimes the input we receive is good and healthy but often it is not.

Labels affect us and in order to determine their influence we must take an honest look at them and separate the truth from the lies about who we are. While I was being abused during my junior high years of school, my peers often labeled me as "scum." This was based on my outward appearance. The clothing I wore was rarely in good condition and I was only allowed to bathe once a week. My peers lacked the understanding of my circumstances, as did my teachers. I heard the comment that I was weird even from a couple of adults. My mother, in her lack of knowledge of the circumstances, labeled me as rebellious and my abuser labeled me as stupid.

I wish I could say none of these characterizations bothered me but of course they did. The important thing that I have learned is to remember that when others are labeling me, they are doing it through the lens with which they see the world and have determined their own identity. If they do not have a healthy view of who they are, they are more likely to project that onto others through the use of labels.

We are just as guilty of labeling ourselves as others are though. For years my self-classifications included abused, broken, worthless and hopeless. Self-labeling is as harmful to us as that we are subjected to by others, if not more so. If you are wondering why that might be so, it is partially because we can't get away from ourselves. We can usually walk away and ignore what others say about us but our brains have no escape from the narrative we are constantly telling them. So, if we have identified with a label that was placed on us and we tell ourselves it is true, our brains will believe us. Our belief will then determine how we respond based on the label we have identified with. If this is a struggle for you, refer back to chapter five on retraining.

Oftentimes we are also subjected to mis-labeling. This occurs when someone identifies a positive character trait as a negative one. For example, you may be called stubborn when really you are determined, hardheaded when you are persistent, bossy when you are strategic, or difficult when you are independent. Every positive character trait can be misinterpreted in a negative light which is why self-awareness regarding our strengths, talents, and skills is so important.

When we are subjected to others defining us in this manner, there are several ways we can respond. First, we can just outright reject what someone says about us and refuse to allow it to influence us. This may or may not be a good response depending on the circumstances. We can also overcompensate somehow in an effort to prove them wrong or change their perception of who we are. Or, if there is nothing we can do to change what others think of us, we may just accept the label even if it is untrue.

For the best outcome we should take time to examine how those around us label us, looking for the lies we have believed about ourselves and exchanging those for the truth. Even if a particular negative label is accurate, we can do something about that. We can change our behavior and our thought processes. Instead of allowing ourselves to be wrapped up in what others say about us or defining ourselves by what we do, whether it is good or bad, we can learn to walk in the identity God has for us when we discover who He is and who He has created us to be.

Chapter Eight Journal Prompts:

What have you learned about your own identity from this chapter?

____

____

____

____

____

What are some of the labels other people have tried to place on you?

____

____

____

____

____

What labels have you placed on yourself? Which labels do you think have been most damaging to you emotionally?

____

____

____

____

____

9.

The Nature of God

For our 20th wedding anniversary, my husband and I decided to have a vow renewal ceremony. Life had been challenging and we needed something good to focus on. However, I was planning it on a broken shoestring budget. In the midst of my planning season for our event, we were invited to the home of our small group leaders. They said they just wanted to have us over for brunch and that it would just be us and them, not our entire small group.

It felt a little like we were getting called to the principal's office, in the nicest possible way, and I agonized all the way up to the day of the event trying to figure out what I had done wrong. When we arrived, it seemed incredibly odd to me that the husband was in the driveway working on his vehicle. I was encouraged by both he and my husband to go on into the house where I discovered a host of friends who had gathered to throw me a surprise "wedding" shower. They knew our circumstances and went above and beyond. They had bought me a new dress for the occasion and provided us with a budget for new clothes for our children's wardrobe for the ceremony as well. Because I hadn't yet fully experienced my healing, the lens with which I viewed the world led me to expect that I was going to be reprimanded. Instead, I was showered with love.

We often approach God in this same manner, feeling as if we are going to be punished for no good reason. But if we will be courageous in drawing near to Him, we will often discover that He really desires to bless us. He is a God of love.

Before we can fully understand what it means to walk in the identity God has for us, we must understand the nature of God. He is distinctively three individuals in one, a triune being consisting of God the Father, Jesus the Son, and Holy Spirit the Counselor. Having a basic concept of how God functions and operates in each of these roles is necessary for us to become who He created us to be.

The scope of the topic of His nature is vast and could be a book all on its own. For the purposes of this book, we will be limiting our exploration of His nature to what is pertinent to our discussion of walking in freedom, identity and purpose after sexual abuse, exploitation and trauma. Once you have this basic understanding, I encourage you to keep learning about the fullness of God's character through Bible reading and Bible studies.

God the Father

Recognizing God as a good father is often a challenge and a stretch for those of us who have been abandoned, neglected, or abused by our dads or other father figures in our lives. Knowing His nature can be elusive when we are not familiar with His word spoken to us throughout the work of the Bible. Trusting Him as a good father can be difficult when we are still wondering why bad things happen in this world. (We discussed this in Truth #6 found in Chapter 4, Recognition.)

Furthermore, discovering the goodness of God will be hard-won at times as we face spiritual warfare and battles. Satan does not want you to live in the fullness of what God has for you and will do whatever he can to convince you that God is not who He says He is. The Bible tells us Satan is a thief who "comes only to steal and kill and destroy…" but goes on to say that God sent Jesus for us "that [we] may have life, and have it to the full." John 10:10. I urge you to keep seeking to understand the loving, good nature of God the Father. The only way the enemy ever wins is if we give up. Do not give up!! Your healing and wholeness are worth the effort. You are worth the effort!!!

So, what are the roles of good fathers? They are providers who secure for us the things we need, shelter, security, stability. Good fathers are ones who have our best interests at heart and go to great lengths to meet our needs. Consider what Matthew 6:26 reveals to us: "Look at the birds of the air; they do not sow or reap or store away in barns, and yet your Heavenly Father feeds them. Are you not much more valuable than they?" God is a good Father who provides for us in every way possible, including the means to overcome a painful and traumatic past.

Good fathers are also teachers who guide us in how to navigate life. Not only has God left us an instruction manual with the Bible, He has provided an example for us in Jesus and He places other Christians in our lives to help us find our way. Psalm 32:8 reveals this truth about God to us: "I will instruct you and teach you in the way you should go; I will counsel you with my loving eye on you."

Good fathers are always available, even when we have strained our relationship with them or are angry at them. Consider Psalm 139:7-10: "Where can I go from your Spirit? Where can I flee from your presence? If I go up to the heavens, you are there; if I make my bed in the depths, you are there. If I rise on the wings of the dawn, if I settle on the far side of the sea, even there your hand will guide me, your right hand will hold me fast." There is no where we can run to or go to hide where our Heavenly Father is not. If you have ever turned your back on Him out of fear, disappointment, or resentment over your trauma like I did, He is there waiting for you to reach out to Him.

While there are many more roles of a good father, the last one I want us to explore at this time is that of an encourager. Good fathers encourage us by proclaiming the depths of their love for us. They reveal to us our value and they help us to nurture and develop our character and talents. When we fail, they encourage us to learn from our mistakes and reassure us that we are capable of accomplishing more and becoming better. My favorite verse about God's encouragement is found in 1 Peter 5:10, I know I used it once before, but it is worth repeating here: "And the God of all grace, who called you to His eternal glory in Christ, after you have suffered a little while, will Himself restore you and make you strong, firm and steadfast."

If understanding God as a good father has been a challenge for you, I hope you are beginning to be able to see the truth. He loves you and desires to instruct, encourage, and provide for you. He is always available to you, He is simply waiting for you to reach out to Him. We have just barely scratched the surface of uncovering His nature in these paragraphs. There is so much more for us to learn about Him, regardless of how long we have been a Christian. As we move forward with this basic understanding of God the Father, I encourage you to dig deeper when you are able.

Jesus the Son

One of the best-known verses of the Bible explains both God's great love for us and Jesus' main purpose for our lives. "For God so loved the world that He gave His one and only Son, that whoever believes in Him shall not perish but have eternal life." John 3:16 Jesus' role in our lives is that of both Savior and example. He lived a sinless life but was crucified as an atonement for our sin. Then He was resurrected to live with the Father in heaven and intercede for us. If you are reading this book, chances are you have accepted Jesus as your Lord and Savior. If not, please continue reading to gain a better understanding of what this means and why it is important in becoming who you were meant to be.

A savior is someone who rescues those in danger. As imperfect people prone to sin, we were in need of rescue and the work Jesus did on the cross provided that for us. The Bible tells us "for all have fallen short of the glory of God, and all are justified freely by His grace through redemption that came by Christ Jesus." Romans 3:23. We were ALL in need of deliverance from evil, so God made a way for us to be rescued. Salvation is a gift from God extended to us when we confess our need for a savior and place our trust in Jesus Christ as such. Once we have made this confession of faith, we are changed, and the identity we once had no longer exists in Christ. "The old has gone, the new is here!" 2 Corinthians 5:17. It is this relationship with Jesus that allows us to step into being all God has created us to be.

Jesus was also given to us as an example of how to live. People had lost sight of the heart of God and what it meant to live in right relationship with Him, so Jesus came as a high priest to lead by example. His leadership was built on loving and serving others. He disrupted the social norms by pointing out the flaws of man-made laws and traditions and called those who heard the sound of His voice to repentance.

Being like Jesus is never easy. It calls for us to lay aside our desires to be right and our right to be vindicated. Becoming Christlike involves surrender which is no easy feat for the one who has been victimized. But I can tell you that every battle I have fought to be who Jesus has called me to be has been worth it. I fully believe that as you determine to overcome what you have been through, your fight will be worth it too.

As we press into the uncomfortableness of trusting Jesus with our life, we will begin to see who He has created us to be. We will discuss these aspects of our new identity in Christ more in the next chapter.

The Holy Spirit

The function of the Holy Spirit at work in our life is to counsel and comfort us. Just as God sent Jesus the Son, Jesus asked God to send the Holy Spirit to us for the sake of teaching us and guiding us. It is the Holy Spirit which empowers us to understand the scriptures and apply them to our lives. Anytime we examine something from our past, it is the Holy Spirit who is the source of wisdom and revelation helping us to discern the truth about it.

What we especially need to know on our journey to freedom and wholeness is that as followers of Jesus Christ, God imparts His spirit to us as the Holy Spirit. The Holy Spirit is the spirit of God that dwells with us to open our eyes to the hope and inheritance we have in Christ. As you seek understanding about how to overcome the pain of your past, the Holy Spirit will empower you to see the truth and understand the new identity you have received from Jesus; "...for it is God who works in you to will and to act in order to fulfill his good purpose." Philippians 2:13

God has a good plan for you and for your life. His character is to provide good things for you, to teach you through the example of Jesus Christ and encourage and empower you to walk in freedom through the power of the Holy Spirit at work in you. Now that we have examined the nature of God, let's get back to discovering our true identity.

Chapter Nine Journal Prompts:

What did you learn about God in this chapter?

____

____

____

____

____

How would you describe your relationship with God at this time?

____

____

____

____

____

10.

Our True Identity

For those of you who may have wondered if Cherry was my real name, it is. Not only is it my name, but my mom's, my grandmother's, and my great-great grandmother's name. But the family name doesn't end with me. I have passed it on to my daughter and she passed it onto hers. To avoid confusion over the years, alternating generations were known by their middle name. However, my daughter decided she also wanted to be known by Cherry.

I can't tell you how much confusion this has caused when people called the house, (back in the day when landlines were common), or at the doctor's office. We got good at asking which Cherry they were referring to when we were called. We were also adept at providing additional identifying information when calling businesses where we both had accounts.

I am grateful that my identity in Christ is much simpler. He knows me intimately, not just by name, and He knows you as well. We never have to verify who we are with Him. But sometimes we need reminders of who we are in Him. Knowing who we are in Christ helps us to remain firmly rooted in His truth and far less likely to fall back into old patterns of behaving or ways of thinking.

It also frees us from the labels and expectations of others and allows us to live a life of purpose.

We began our journey addressing how the issue of shame shapes the lens we view ourselves through. We took a look at the labels often placed on us and how damaging they are to us. And we explored all of the attributes that typically factor into our concept of identity. I would also like to note here, that when sexual abuse, trauma, or exploitation happen at an early age, the development of a survivor's identity is often stunted. One's emotional growth can become stagnant and underdeveloped as she continues to mature physically.

With these things in mind, it is no wonder that believing we are worthy of love from others, from ourselves, and even from God is challenging. Hopefully by now you are beginning to realize hope is available to you and that it is possible to step into the identity God has for you: free of shame, fully loved, and facing a future of potential. So let's take a closer look at who God says we are.

#1 We are God's creation.

God created the earth and everything in it, including us. But the Bible tells us that God took special care with man and woman making "mankind in His image." "So God created mankind in His own image, in the image of God He created them; male and female He created them." Genesis 1:27

Being made in His image and being a reflection of who He is, just as children are a reflection of their parents, invites us to be in relationship with Him. We are His creation, formed in our mother's womb. He knit together every detail of our physical and personality traits. We are not an accident. We were "fearfully and wonderfully made" with the utmost care and attention.

He knew us before we were born because He designed us to be His beloved child. We are the workmanship of His hands. More than any earthly parent ever could, He wanted us and made us in such a way that we could relate to Him. "For you created my inmost being, you knit me together in my mother's womb. I praise you because I am fearfully and wonderfully made; your works are wonderful, I know that full well." Psalm 139:13-14

We must allow the truth that we are God's creation to penetrate the depths of our self-concept and learn to perceive who we are through the lens of His word. Studying His word will reveal to us how we are to interact with those around us. It also reminds us that God's truth about us is far more important than anyone else's opinion of us, including our own. When we are rooted in Christ, our self-awareness should point us back to our need for Jesus and remind us that He is our creator.

#2 We have become children of God through Jesus.

Even though sin entered the world through Adam and Eve, and we were born into a life of sin, God made a way for us to become His children forever through His son Jesus Christ. "Yet to all who did receive Him, to those who believed in his name, He gave the right to become children of God-." John 1:12.

He loved us so much that He provided a way for us to experience knowing Him and walking with Him here in this life and for eternity. That way is through our faith in Jesus as our Lord and Savior. "In Him we have redemption through His blood, the forgiveness of sins, in accordance with the riches of God's grace." Ephesians 1:7.

So if we believe, then we are indeed God's children and inheritors of every good spiritual gift, from healing to freedom, that He has for us. As children of God we are cared for and deeply loved by a good Father who longs for us to seek Him and the path He has for us.

Self-confidence becomes more of a God-confidence that radiates from the knowledge that we are His and we are deeply loved. This new confidence in who we are in Christ should change the way we see ourselves and how we interact with the world around us. As we grow in the assurance of who we are to God, we will also experience greater peace than we ever did relying on our own self-confidence.

If you do not know God as your Father and if you have never before declared faith in Jesus Christ as the Son of God and your Savior and you would like to do so now, please refer to the resource section of this book where you will find a simple prayer to pray for forgiveness and salvation. Walking out life as a child of God is where peace, joy, hope, purpose, and freedom begin.

#3 We are capable.

For a long time, I wasn't sure that I would ever be free from the baggage of my trauma. I didn't know if the resulting wounds would heal. And honestly, I spent many years working in my own strength to try to make that happen. Ultimately, I just ended up feeling like I was beating my head against a brick wall. It wasn't until I was willing to allow God to start tearing that wall down and expose the foundations of what I needed to deal with that I began to really find healing.

In Matthew 19:21-26 Jesus and the disciples are having a conversation about spiritual salvation that I believe is applicable to our spiritual healing as well. We have to give up what we are hanging onto in order to receive what God has for us. Many of us have spent so much time letting our trauma define us that it is difficult to let go of it. I believe when we are truly ready to allow God to guide us into freedom, we are capable of accomplishing that through Him. "With man this is impossible, but with God all things are possible." Matthew 19:26

While the Cambridge Dictionary tells us that being capable means we have the ability to do things well and achieve results,[4] Romans 8:37 reveals that "we are more than conquerors through him who loved us" and Philippians 4:13 echoes that we "can do all things through [Christ]." Being in relationship with God through His son Jesus is fundamentally what makes us capable of overcoming our pasts.

____

[4] https://dictionary.cambridge.org/us/dictionary/english/capable accessed 3/3/23

Pursuing a relationship with the Lord will usually require us to reassess our values. Do the things we give our time and attention to line up with what we are taught in the Bible? As we learn more about what it means to follow Jesus and as we learn to deeply rely on the Holy Spirit, we become more competent in our ability to align our values with those of God the Father. Our capabilities will grow from being able to overcome our pasts to being able to pursue our God-given hopes and dreams.

#4 We have purpose.

Wondering about who we are and why we exist is not uncommon. Many people often contemplate whether or not their life has purpose. The good news for us is that God tells us in His word that we are valuable, and our lives do indeed have purpose. "For we are God's handiwork, created in Christ Jesus to do good works, which God prepared in advance for us to do." Ephesians 2:19.

I am in awe when I take in a beautiful sunset or sunrise, or when I sit on the beach and watch the waves crash. I am often breathless when I look up at the sky on a crystal clear night. God's handiwork takes my breath away. Everything He created He designed to reveal His glory. And you are counted in His handiwork. You have been created to know the wonders of who your Creator is and to make those known to others.

In the simplest of terms, the core of our identity is to know God and make Him known to others. This purpose is a universal principle that applies to everyone. Every person God created, He created to serve His purpose and plans, but He has a specific path for each of us to follow while doing so. My opinion is that those of us who pursue the Lord and His plans, find the peace, contentment and freedom He has for us. Those individuals who chase fame, fortune, success or relationships as a means to find fulfillment are usually left deeply disappointed.

This general purpose for our life seems simple, but God has created each one of us so uniquely that we each also have a distinct purpose in life. His unique plans for our lives include all of our traits, talents, skills, and even experiences that we have. When we surrender these things back to Him, we are prepared to do the work He has for us to do.

We will address our individual purposes more in depth in the following chapters but for now let's press into knowing Him, learning about His nature and His love for us. Leaning into the purpose of knowing God as Father, Son and Spirit, is a worthy pursuit that will help ground you in the identity He has for you. "But you are a chosen people, a royal priesthood, a holy nation, God's special possession, that you may declare the praises of Him who called you out of darkness into his wonderful light." 1 Peter 2:9.

#5 We are loved and accepted.

God's love for us is unconditional and He accepts us completely through our confession of Jesus as our Lord and Savior. Our pasts have no bearing on how much God loves us. He displayed the depths of His love and care for us when He sent Jesus to die on the cross as an eternal sacrifice for our sins. He longs to be in relationship with us because we are His beloved children. "See what great love the Father has lavished on us, that we should be called children of God! And that is what we are!" 1 John 3:1.

Not long ago, my six-year-old granddaughter wanted to do a magic trick for her granddad. She stood before him, holding something in her hands and told him to say abracadabra. He said something else instead so she explained to him that was not right and repeated the directions to say the magic word. Again, he said something silly and she was about to give up on him when he told her he would do it right. For the third time she asked him to say abracadabra and once again he failed his assignment.

Then the most amazing thing happened. My sweet little granddaughter let out a big sigh and said, "Okay, say what you're going to say and then I'm going to do my magic trick." I mentioned that she was six right? But even at such a young age, she has such a deep love for her grandfather that she was willing to overlook his orneriness and share her love for him by doing her trick. She didn't see just his failures and mistakes. She saw the man who is fun, loving, and dotes on her so she responded with compassion.

We tend to think that our flaws and failures, our quirks and idiosyncrasies, our stubbornness, weaknesses, and mistakes will drive God away. But similar to the love my granddaughter has for my husband, God's love for us is unyielding. It is far better than any human love or affection. His love for us will never fail and He will never abandon us. We see this in Deuteronomy 31:6: "Be strong and courageous. Do not be afraid or terrified because of them, *for the LORD your God goes with you; He will never leave you nor forsake you*." (Emphasis mine.)

Our identity as children of God is wrapped up in our confession of faith in Jesus as the Son of God and who God intends us to be. Through these things we are identified as God's creation and His children who are capable of overcoming our pasts and living a life purpose because we are loved by Him. Whatever we were before and whatever labels were assigned to us no longer have meaning in our lives.

My hope and prayer is that you can embrace the identity God has for you and that as you do, you will experience healing, joy, and hope in fresh new ways. It is my deepest desire that understanding your identity will help propel you into living out the distinct purpose God has for you. Let the labels of "loved" and "accepted" carry more weight than any other classification that has ever been placed on you. Take note that "if anyone is in Christ, the new creation has come: The old has gone, the new is here!" 2 Corinthians 5:17.

Chapter Ten Journal Prompts:

How do you see yourself in comparison to who God says you are?

____

____

____

____

____

____

Which of the concepts outlined in this chapter are most challenging for you to believe or accept? Why do you think that is so?

____

____

____

____

____

Discovering Your Specific Purpose

11.

Where Purpose Begins

Shellfish are a category of marine and freshwater animals that include mollusks like clams, oysters, and mussels, as well as many forms of crustaceans. In general clams, oysters, and mussels have a purpose which is important to the wellbeing of aquatic environments. They help filter harmful algae and particles from the water.

However, when one of these mollusks encounters foreign objects and irritants entering their body, an immune response is initiated. A "pearl sac" is formed around the source of the irritation. Chemicals are then secreted which cover the sac and harden, trapping the foreign body inside. Over the course of several months or even several years, this process is repeated again and again, until eventually a precious pearl is formed.

While pearls may vary in size, shape, color and quality, they all have a lustrous and reflective, although not perfect, finish. Pearls are highly valued for their rarity and beauty. Natural pearls are the only gems created by living creatures and they have been used throughout the centuries in the creation of beautiful jewelry pieces and adornments.

When something negative, unpleasant, uncomfortable, or even traumatic happens in our lives, we can take a lesson from the shellfish that produce pearls. First, we should immediately encapsulate the "irritant" injecting itself into our life in prayer. Then we should begin to apply God's truth to it, over and over again if necessary, until something treasured is created.

Just like natural pearls, it may take months or years for "spiritual pearls" to take shape in our lives. Examples of spiritual pearls might be forgiveness, perseverance, compassion, wisdom, understanding, kindness, patience, or powerful testimonies about what we have overcome in our lives. Regardless of what is cultivated in us, these gems become a part of our specific purpose and are meant to be a reflection of God's transformative ability.

What makes our pearls valuable is how He has taken something meant to harm us and turned it into a thing of purpose. When we have developed the ability to say "You intended to harm me, but God intended it for good to accomplish what is now being done..." (Genesis 50:20) we can know we are ready to walk out God's precise purpose in our own lives.

Prayer

This kind of knowledge about our identity and purpose is developed over time through the practice of prayer. Prayer is foundational to growing in our relationship with the Lord. It is one of the most important and powerful spiritual disciplines we can establish in our lives. Since it is an essential key to knowing God better and knowing His purpose for our lives, let me spend some time expanding upon how to build an effective prayer life by answering a few questions about prayer.

What is prayer?

When people are asked "what is prayer?" a common response is "talking to God". While this is an accurate answer it is also an incomplete one. Prayer is much more than that. Prayer is a conversation with God. Conversations are a dialogue in which the participants listen and respond to one another. Therefore prayer is a dialogue with God in which we are expressing our hearts to Him, and listening for His response to us.

Communication is also the means by which relationships grow and develop. Think about it, how close are you to people you don't interact with? And how do you feel when someone rattles off a whole list of what is going on in their life but never stops to allow you to comment? Life probably feels pretty lopsided under these circumstances, doesn't it?

I know there was a time in my life when my exchanges with God resembled those things. I went days, or weeks, sometimes even longer, without taking the time to engage in prayer. Then, very often when I did, it was one-sided with me telling God about all my problems but never listening for His perspective or response. This approach left me wondering why I wasn't growing in my faith the way I thought I should be. Praying without listening for God's response is often ineffective at bringing about change in our lives.

Prayer is the foundational spiritual discipline, partnered with reading the Bible, that will allow you to build a relationship with the Lord and grow in your faith.

Why Is Prayer Important?

We began to answer this question of why prayer is important while discussing what prayer is, pointing out that it is the foundation of our relationship with the Lord. Let's take a minute to examine that point a bit more. The more we talk to others and listen to what they have to say, the better we get to know them. The same holds true for our conversations with God. The more we share with Him and the more we receive what He has to say, the better we know Him.

Knowing Him is one of the primary purposes God has for our lives. He sent Jesus to sacrifice His life so that we might have a relationship with God the Father, through our belief in Jesus as the son of God. The work Jesus did for us through His death, burial and resurrection solidifies that purpose in our lives. A consistent, ongoing prayer life is essential to knowing and understanding God better.

Prayer was an important part of Jesus' earthly life. It was what empowered Him to live sinlessly and complete His assignment to die for our sins. Apart from His relationship with God the Father, He would not have been able to do so. He himself states in John 5:19 "Very truly I tell you, the Son can do nothing by Himself; He can do only what he sees his Father doing, because whatever the Father does the Son also does."

God has a plan and a purpose for our lives that cannot be accomplished without us being in relationship with Him. Being in relationship with Him requires that we are in communication with Him through prayer. Just as Jesus set the example of prayer for us throughout the New Testament, Paul also tells us Philippians 4:9 "Whatever you have learned or received or heard from me, or seen in me—put it into practice. And the God of peace will be with you."

As we practice the discipline of prayer, "the God of peace will be with" us. In and of ourselves, we can accomplish nothing, but through our relationship, which is built on prayer and His word, we can experience wholeness, healing, forgiveness, hope and peace. Only then can we fulfill the purposes He has for us.

How Often Should We Pray?

Should prayer be a one-and-done event for the day, the week, the month or just for special occasions? Absolutely not. Remember that prayer is conversation. What would happen if you only had one conversation a day with those you live with? Would your relationship continue to grow or would it begin to falter? Most likely, without communication, you would find yourself drifting away from those in your home.

So, how often should we pray then? The Bible gives us two answers in particular that we should look at. The first is found in one of the simplest verses of the Bible: 1 Thessalonians 5:17: "pray continually." We are to pray constantly, all throughout the day.

Just as we might stop to send our loved ones a text in the middle of the day, we can stop to communicate with the Lord. We can express our gratitude, ask for guidance, lift up the needs of someone else and even let Him know what we think about a situation or how we feel. This continual communication helps us become more aware of His presence that is always with us.

So in light of the fact we are called to pray all the time, you might be wondering what the second answer to our question is. Let's take a glance at Mark 1:35: "Very early in the morning, while it was still dark, Jesus got up, left the house, and went off to a solitary place, where He prayed." Jesus prayed at an appointed time. He made room for time in His day to pray in a place where He would not be distracted.

I realize that some of you just read "early in the morning" and felt your heart sink. Maybe you are just not a morning person. Maybe you are, but you are also a mom of little ones who get up very early. Let me just say this, an appointed time does not have to be the wee hours of the morning. God created you so He understands the rhythms of your life and He gives grace for that and He will honor your efforts. But, if you want to continue to know Him more, and you want to keep moving forward with your spiritual growth, you must have appointed times of prayer.

What does an appointed time of prayer look like? Most often we think of a prayer meeting at church or in Sunday service and while corporate prayer is invaluable, we need to have planned moments everyday that we can meet with the Lord. The time of day is not nearly as important as setting aside time that will be uninterrupted and free of distractions.

So what does that look like for you? Is it after the kids go to bed? Is it first thing in the morning? Do you need to lock yourself in your car, away from the world on your lunch break? Do what works for you, but make a plan, put it on your schedule and stick to it. Having a fulfilling prayer life is not about the time or the place, it's about the commitment. "Be joyful in hope, patient in affliction, faithful in prayer." Romans 12:12.

Does God Speak to Us?

Absolutely! A. W. Tozier once wrote "It is the nature of God to speak." Does that mean that we hear His audible voice? Sometimes people do hear the voice of God. At other times though, God speaks to us through what we see and experience. But, we must first be mindful that God communicates with us in numerous ways. We just have to be aware of God's presence and be willing to listen.

God can speak to us through music, sermons, situations, art, and creation. He speaks to us through sunsets, stories, friends, loved ones, and even strangers. The question is: "are we paying attention?" As we develop the ability to hear God speaking to us, we can be assured that we are accurately hearing from Him by examining a few things about what we have heard. The first is if it lines up with what is written in the Bible. God does not contradict Himself.

If what we have heard is contradictory to the Biblical principles found in God's word, then it's not from Him. I would encourage you, that if you are ever in any doubt, seek out a trusted friend or spiritual leader who can help you sort through the truth of what you are hearing.

Additionally, the Lord is very good at doing what needs to be done to get our attention. If you hear something on Sunday at church, hear it again on the radio, then read it in a book, or the same subject comes up some other way, chances are God is speaking to you through repetition. Pay attention and then pray for wisdom about what you've heard. "Ask, and it will be given to you; seek, and you will find; knock, and the door will be opened to you." Matthew 7:7.

Being equipped with the knowledge of how prayer plays a role in building a relationship with God will propel you forward in identifying His specific purpose for your life.

Chapter Eleven Journal Prompts:

How can you build upon the practice of prayer you currently have?

____

____

____

____

____

____

In what ways do you most often sense God speaking to you?

____

____

____

____

____

____

12.

Discovery

We touched on God's general purpose for everyone in a previous chapter. Now let's take a look at discovering His specific purpose for us personally. Purpose is the reason for which God created you to exist. It is accomplished by living a life surrendered to Jesus and using all of the gifts, talents and experiences we have for the glory of God. There are several components to finding the specific purpose God has for you. Most importantly determining your purpose will take wisdom that comes from God. As you look at each of the pieces in learning how to discover the tasks God has for you to carry out, ask Him to give you insight concerning each of them.

Know who you are in Christ.

We spent time in the previous chapter learning about our identity. There are a couple of benefits you will experience when you are firmly planted in the knowledge of who you are in Jesus and how that relates to the path you are on.

First, understanding your identity through Him takes the pressure of perfection and performance off of you. It frees you from the burden of trying to accomplish His mission for your life in your own strength. God is not nearly as interested in the outcome as He is in your obedience and ability to trust Him. Not only has God made you capable to do what He calls you to do, but He has also equipped you:

"And God is able to bless you abundantly, so that in all things at all times, having all that you need, you will abound in every good work." 2 Corinthians 9:8.

An additional benefit of knowing who and whose you are is gaining stability. When your feet are firmly planted in the truth of God's word about your identity, it prevents your emotions and imaginations from derailing you. When you lose sight of who you are, worry and doubt often begin to creep in and steal your peace. If you start to experience this anxious restlessness, remember that we are to "demolish arguments and every pretension that sets itself up against the knowledge of God, and we take captive every thought to make it obedient to Christ." 2 Corinthians 10:5.

We also live in a world that often freely offers their opinions about who they think we are. In the pages of this book, we have talked about how harmful labels can be and the emotional turmoil they can stir up. As you walk in faith following Jesus, you may find that the world will continue to try to label you. This is when it is vital to remember what God says about you. By focusing on whose you are, you can overcome the temptation to allow the labels, attitudes and opinions of those around you to define you. As you discard the old labels from the world, and put on the labels your Heavenly Father has for you. If we know that we know that "...God is for us, [then] who can be against us?" Romans 8:31

Finally, when you can comprehend the completeness and the fullness of the Father's love for us, you will have confidence in who God has created you to be and what He has prepared for you to accomplish. You can be assured knowing that your identity and relationship with the Lord are secure and unchanging. Nothing "in all creation, will be able to separate us from the love of God that is in Christ Jesus our Lord." Romans 8:39

Know what you love to do and what you are good at.

I love to sing in worship services. I don't sing anywhere else because I can't really carry a tune very well. Because of this, I am forever grateful that Psalm 98 tells us that we are to make a joyful noise instead of telling us to sing a beautiful song. There are many things that we might enjoy doing but that doesn't mean those things are our mission assignment. Trust me, no one wants me to join the choir.

So in uncovering your specific purpose you must look for the things that you both love doing AND are skilled at implementing. What have your skills, talents and experiences prepared you for? Remember that nothing is wasted in God's economy. Ephesians 2:10 tells us that we were created "to do good works, which God prepared in advance for us to do." God has prepared something for each of us and in that preparation He has given us the ability to enjoy what we do.

Does that mean it will always be fun or easy? I don't think so and that has not been the experience of anyone I know. However, it does mean that we will be able to enjoy the results of our work and find satisfaction in it, even when it's hard. I encourage you to make a list of what you love doing and what you can do really well. Look to see where those things intersect and how they might be of benefit to those around you.

Know who you are called to serve and what they need.

Once you have determined those things you both enjoy and excel at, it's time to take a look at who you are drawn to helping. What needs do you see everywhere you go? Who are the people whose circumstances break your heart? Who do you have something you can offer? Children, parents, homeless, special needs families, those recovering from addictions, the disabled, veterans? Involve the Lord in this process and ask Him to reveal to you the issues you are passionate about. It may not always be what you think.

When my children were small, we discovered one of them had an Autism Spectrum Disorder. I began to meet parent after parent with children on the spectrum and hear story after story of how these families were not welcomed in church. When I approached my pastor and told him about the needs I saw, he asked me "How can we help you serve the needs of those you are meeting?" I wasn't looking for it, and I didn't even feel especially equipped for it, but God pointed me in the direction of a specific purpose for that season of my life.

I served as a Special Needs Ministry Coordinator for 5 years because I had a passion to help other special needs families have access to church and respite care. God used the compassion I felt in conjunction with my experiences as a parent of a special needs child and my ability to organize and coordinate events to meet a need in our community. I wasn't expecting that or even wanting to do that at the time. I share this with you to encourage you to be open to the leading of the Holy Spirit even as you examine the practical aspects of living a life of purpose.

Your specific purpose may change from time to time but ultimately, the greatest gift of value we can offer is Jesus. Find a way to serve the people that God points out to you, with the skills, talents, abilities and interests He has given you, in a way that meets their practical needs and points them back to a relationship with God. This is what it looks like to walk in the specific purpose God has for you in whatever season you are in.

Know how their lives could be changed through your service to them.

Crucial to serving others well is knowing how their lives can be changed by what you offer them. The specific assignment God has for your life at any given time is not about you. It is about bringing Him glory and helping others come to a saving knowledge of Jesus as their Lord and Savior. It's about continuing to help them live out a life of hope and freedom. It's about sharing what God has done in your life with others who desperately need it. It's about helping others to continue growing in their relationship with the Lord.

Know that the work you do for God should have eternity at the heart of it.

Understand that when you serve others you reflect the love of Jesus Christ to them. How you minister and care for them, even in the smallest and simplest of ways, can be deeply meaningful to them and have a lasting impact on their life.

So let me take these four things and put them into an example for you. In this season of my life I know that I know that I am a daughter of the King of Kings. I have been redeemed, healed, set free, and I am a joint heir with Christ. This is who I am. This is my identity. I love to write and create and encourage others and my heart breaks for other women who have experienced sexual abuse, assault and exploitation. I know that the healing I have experienced through my relationship with Jesus is valuable and that by sharing my story, other women may also find their healing, freedom, identity and purpose. This is my specific mission calling and purpose in this season of my life.

Assessments to help you determine your spiritual gifts and personal strengths may be helpful on your journey of discovering who God created you to be and what He has for you to do. In the resource section at the end of this book you will find links for the ones I have used and liked. I do caution you to take care with personality evaluations. While some have more legitimacy than others, it is always best to rely on the Lord and the Bible to define who you are.

I encourage you to start with these principles above combined with the counsel of the Holy Spirit to understand how your gifts, talents and personality traits relate to the purpose God has for your life. And if it takes you a while to figure it out, that's okay. God knows where you are in the process and His timing is perfect. As you're learning, jump in and serve wherever you see a need. The experience will be helpful not just to those around you, but also in your own personal journey of discovery and healing.

Chapter Twelve Journal Prompts:

What can you do today to help you better understand your unique purpose?

____

____

____

____

____

Make a list of friends, coworkers, and family members you can ask to help you identify some of your strengths and talents:

____

____

____

____

____

13.

Destination Freedom

On the second day of my seminary classes I was having a discussion with God during my drive over to the campus. I'd had the same conversion with him the day I went for student orientation and the first day of class. I was wrestling with how it could be the right time for me to start college. There were so many other things going on in my life that seemed not only daunting, but limiting and prohibitive.

I got to class, sat in the front row of my Life of Jesus class and the professor started off with a lesson in context surrounding an incredibly well known and often quoted scripture used as encouragement: Jeremiah 29:11 "For I know the plans I have for you," declares the Lord, "plans to prosper you and not to harm you, plans to give you hope and a future."

If we look at Jeremiah 29:4-14 we discover that God is speaking to His children, the Israelites, who have been carried off into exile by the Babylonians. There was a prophet among them that had told them lies that all their troubles would be short lived, (see Jeremiah 28). God is correcting that misconception and explaining to them that they will be in exile for 70 years. Furthermore, He is calling them to do life while they are there. Then comes the promise of plans for freedom, prosperity and hope. These are followed by the assurance that as we seek Him through the process of doing life in the hard times, we will find Him.

I wept as I sat in the front row of that class because it was exactly what I needed to hear from God at that moment to be encouraged to continue on the path He had set for me. I'd like to suggest you take time to read Jeremiah 29:4-14 and ask God what He has to reveal to you personally through them.

In a sense, we were carried into captivity by the actions of our abusers. But even in the midst of being held hostage by our pasts, God has a plan for our lives to bring us into freedom. In the context of the discussion we've been having about overcoming shame and finding that freedom, there are three things I think we can take from these verses of Jeremiah and additional scriptures to apply to our lives.

- Do Life, even when it's hard. Don't give up! It may not get easier right away but if you are walking through challenges while in relationship with the Lord, He will encourage you and establish your path. (1 Peter 5:10)
- Lean on God. Trust that He sees you exactly where you are and that He will be with you every step of the way. Believe His word that says He is working in all things for your good. (Romans 8:28)
- Make Plans. Have a vision for the direction you are going in. Without a plan and a vision, failure is almost inevitable. "Where there is no vision, the people perish." Proverbs 29:18a KJV

Even if this book is the first step on your journey to find healing from sexual abuse and trauma, you have already come so far! You have come too far just to set this book on your night stand and go back to the way things were. In light of that, let's put number 3 into action by using MAKE as an acronym for the steps you need to take to continue moving forward towards your restoration. Keep in mind these things are based on the reconstructive model of dealing with shame that you can always refer back to as needed.

M- Make peace with your past.

Remember, life's not fair. What you experienced was hard and heartbreaking. As you allow yourself to experience your emotions, invite God into the process. Ask Him to show you any mistruths or misconceptions you have had about your past and to reveal His truth concerning your circumstances.

Refrain from comparing your story of restoration with that of others. While there are commonalities many abuse victims share, your journey to overcome your past is completely unique to you. Do not allow bitterness or comparison to set in and rob you of your potential and your freedom.

A - Adopt a plan.

To adopt means to follow or use. Consider creating a plan for yourself that you can easily follow to keep you moving forward in your healing. You can use the steps outlined in the reconstructive process as a place to start. Consider including your hopes and dreams in the guide you create, allowing the Holy Spirit to redirect you as needed.

As you are creating a system to help you continue making progress, think about obstacles you may need to remove from your life. They could be bad habits, activities (good or bad), or maybe even people. Now consider what resources you need to add to your plan to help you achieve your goals. Maybe you need to invest in some education, skills training, or additional support. Accountability through counseling, life coaching, or discipleship programs might also be beneficial. Be intentional about setting yourself up for success by adding what you need to your plan.

K - Keep going.

The next step is to keep going. Once you have a plan, implement it. A plan is just a guide until you put it into action. If you want to realize results, you have to carry out your plan. Results come from actually doing something and following through.

If you don't direct your aim at an outcome, you will succeed in not trying. It is much more rewarding to accomplish progress towards your goals. Even if you fail while reaching for your destination, you can always readjust, regroup, redirect and continue to move forward.

E - Enlist help.

Now that you have identified what needs to go, stay, or be added to your plan for you to make progress, find a support group, friend, mentor, coach or counselor that can help you. Remember that you were created for relationships.

When faced with all that we have endured, it is tempting to try to manage recovery on your own. Isolation does not aid the healing process but having a healthy community around you does. While you may eventually find release from the bondage of your experiences doing it by yourself, I can assure you the process will take much longer. Remember, I said I spent 15 years feeling like I was banging my head against a wall in my pursuit of wholeness. It wasn't until I found help that I finally started making progress.

In order to achieve your goal of walking in freedom, identity and purpose, you will need someone who can lovingly hold you accountable to your personal growth and development. Be sure it's someone you trust and are comfortable giving permission to ask you the hard questions. This will be essential in their ability to help you when you get stuck.

As the topic of sexual abuse and exploitation garners more attention, access to resources seems to be increasing. This should make it easier for you to find the help you need to continue the process you have begun. As you look for resources to help you on your journey, consider these four things:

Referrals and recommendations from others you know and trust can be useful. In the absence of a referral I would suggest you do your research on whatever resource you are considering to discern whether or not it will be a good fit for you.

Don't rush the process. It's better to take your time finding an individual or community that you are comfortable with than to be re-traumatized by the first group you land in.

When you do find a person or organization you think might work, don't feel pressured to disclose everything at once. Get to know the people you are sharing with and allow for the opportunity for trust to grow. No one needs to know more than what you are willing to share or sooner than you are ready to tell it.

If you begin to engage with an individual or group and discover that it is not a good fit, do not feel stuck. It is perfectly ok for you to thank them for their time and excuse yourself from the conversation. You should never put yourself in any situation that feels unsafe. Being uncomfortable is sometimes necessary for growth, but only within the confines of trusted relationships.

Be patient with yourself as you look for the right support system but also make finding one a priority. If you get stuck trying to find help, please reach out to me. I'd be honored to assist you.

Chapter Thirteen Journal Prompts:

Using the MAKE acronym, outline your next steps to restoration:

14.

Conclusion

Seven combined years of abuse between my sister and I had been whittled down to just five counts when our abuser was tried in court. For each of these counts he was convicted and sentenced to five years in prison. However, instead of being confined for twenty-five years he was allowed to serve his sentences concurrently, meaning all at the same time, and was released after just five years. Even so, Tammy and I received more justice than most women do. I believe that the majority of offenders are never held accountable for their actions.

When justice is dispensed it means that each person receives what they deserve. As survivors, what we deserve is not necessarily retribution, but it is restoration. Our abusers can never provide this for us. It must be found in walking out our healing and embracing the freedom, identity, and purpose God has for us. In light of this, I think that it is important to reframe our idea of what justice can be. It is possible for it to simply be a life well lived.

A life well lived is one that is no longer imprisoned by the trauma and pain of the past. It is one in which we declare victory over the memories of hurt and pain. It is one in which we reach out to others who are where we have been and help them get to where we are.

In May of 2017, I had the opportunity to share my story with a group of women in the town my mom and sister lived in. I traveled the day before the speaking event to stay the night with them and Tammy decided she wanted to go with me. As I shared not just my story, but our story, she listened intently. After the event she excitedly told me that she also wanted to begin sharing our story to encourage other survivors and that she wanted us to be able to do it together. My heart was overwhelmed with joy at the possibility.

She had come to a place in her life where she understood how very much God loved her. She was healed of bi-polar disorder, multiple personalities, and drug addictions that had all been rooted in her trauma. She was ready to tell everyone about the restoration she had experienced and help them find it too. I can't imagine a better example of living life well.

Tragically, Tammy passed away just nine days later, suddenly and unexpectedly. I'm so grateful that I got to be a part of her healing journey. I hope, that in some small way through the pages of this book, that both she and I have encouraged you to embrace the process of being remade. Every difficult step is worth it. You are worth it.

Resources

Resources

Chapter 10: Our True Identity

Salvation

"May your unfailing love come to me, Lord, your salvation, according to your promise; then I can answer anyone who taunts me, for I trust in your word." Psalm 119:41-42

If you are not yet a follower of Jesus, surrender your heart to Christ with this simple prayer: "Jesus, I need you. I repent for living as if I don't, and I ask for your forgiveness. Please guide me as I commit to surrendering my life to you. Lead me in your truth and salvation. In Jesus Name, Amen."

Now, share with someone the decision you made to become a follower of Christ and find a Bible based church to be a part of. These things are essential to your spiritual growth.

Chapter 11: Where Purpose Begins

For a review of what has been shared about prayer, including The FAITH Model of Prayer and 28 days of journaling pages you can purchase *The Practice of Prayer and Prayer Journaling: Understanding Prayer And The Benefits of Praying Consistently*

@ https://www.amazon.com/dp/B0C5YM25KF

If you need prayer TBN has many trained prayer partners. Just call 1-714-731-1000 or submit a prayer request online at https://www.tbn.org/prayer

Chapter 12: Discovery

There is a vast array of resources available online to help you determine your gifts, talents and strengths. Here are a few of my favorites:

Spiritual Gifts Teaching:

https://www.christianity.com/wiki/christian-life/what-are-spiritual-gifts-understanding-the-types-and-discovering-yours.html

Spiritual Gifts Assessment:

Spiritual-gifts-survey

Strengths Assessment:

https://www.gallup.com/cliftonstrengths/en/252137/home.aspx

National Hotlines

If you picked up this book while you are still in the midst of abuse or you know someone who is in danger or at risk there are several national hotlines that may be of use to you. However, If you are in immediate danger dial 911

The National Sexual Assault Hotline: 800-656-HOPE or you can chat online at https://www.rainn.org/resources . Options for Spanish Speakers are available as well.

The National Domestic Violence Hotline: 800-799-SAFE and the National Center for Victims of Crimes: 855-4-VICTIM

For the sexually exploited and trafficked, the National Human Trafficking Hotline is available at 888-373-7888 or text to 233733. Online: https://humantraffickinghotline.org/en

Chat

As mentioned throughout this book, if you have no one else to chat with, please feel free to text me at 940-368-2793 or email me at cherry@beingremade.org

About the Author

Cherry is trained as Chaplain and life coach and holds an Associate's Degree in Christian Ministries from The King's University. She has a wide variety of ministry experience over the past twenty years that has equipped her to speak into the lives of others. She is the founder of Being Remade, which exists to transform difficult pasts into beautiful futures.

Cherry has a passion to encourage, empower and equip women to embrace the process of being remade into who God intends them to be, especially women who are transitioning from abusive, traumatic, or difficult life circumstances. Her personal testimony about overcoming an abusive childhood was published in the Roaring Lambs book, Stories of Roaring Faith, Volume 3.

Through her work experience at some amazing organizations, Refuge For Women NTX as a shift lead, TBN as a prayer partner, and Program Coach for Flourish Homes, she has been able to pursue her passion to help women discover hope and healing.

Cherry has also written *The Practice of Prayer and Prayer Journaling: Understanding Prayer and The Benefits of Praying Consistently* and created a coloring book, *Blossoms, Blooms & Pollinators: Relaxation Coloring Book for Adults and Teens*. Both can be found on Amazon, and you can connect with Cherry online at www.beingremade.org

Cherry lives in the Tulsa, Oklahoma area with her family. She has four children and several grands. She enjoys being involved in her church and local community. When Cherry is not working, writing, speaking, or teaching she loves being crafty and her favorite thing to create is handmade junk journals.